made to play!

made to play!

Handmade Toys and Crafts for Growing Imaginations

Joel Henriques

ROOST BOOKS · BOSTON & LONDON · 2011

contents

acknowledgments

Special thanks to my wife and children for all of their love and inspiration. To my sister Andra, for telling me I should write a craft book. My sister Lori, for all of her support and expert advice. And everyone else in my entire family. Also, to my editor Jennifer Urban-Brown, for the opportunity, guidance, and encouragement.

introduction

Ever since my kids were born, I've been fascinated by watching how they interact with objects. I started to appreciate how something like a small piece of Velcro on a teething bib would give their six-month-old minds and bodies something to explore for long periods of time. As they got older, I kept seeing examples of how simple toys often gave them more satisfaction and confidence than a toy that was too complicated. I was also amazed at how sophisticated their creativity would be when given the chance to have optional ways to play with a toy. The projects in this book combine my recent experience as a father with my life-long love for toys, art, and simplicity. I hope they will provide you and the kids in your life a bit of fun!

you as a toy maker

These projects are all very adaptable. If you have your own design ideas, then try them! Change the size of a toy, or use different materials. For example, try making the portable zoo animals huge or the wood toys out of cardboard. Do whatever works best for you. Also, when crafting the toys in this book, try to relax about making a straight cut or sewing a straight line—the imperfections in handmade toys are what make them so special. And the real magic of these projects is the bonding process while creating or presenting them.

My Favorite Materials

This book includes projects made from wood, wire, fabric, and paper. Here are some of the tools and materials I prefer.

- **Beeswax Polish.** I use a great all-natural polish by Three BEEautiful Bees. Just rub it into wooden toys with your fingers. The polish is great for the toys and your skin! I don't polish all of my wooden toys with beeswax, as sometimes I like the feel of raw wood. However, if I know it's going to be an outdoor toy, or sucked on by a baby, then I always put beeswax on it to protect the wood.

- **Paint Pens.** I use non-toxic Painters Opaque Paint Markers by Elmer's. They're great for fabric and cardboard, and also for decorating wood toys.

- **Acrylic Paints.** I use a non-toxic acrylic paint by A2 Chroma, which is perfect for making kids' toys.

- **Sandpaper.** I use fine 150-grit sandpaper, followed by a super-fine 400 grit. The 400 grit makes the wood very smooth—perfect for little hands.

- **Scroll Saw.** Scroll saws are great for cutting out small toys. I have a very old one, and you

can often find them used. Jigsaws also work well to make detailed cuts, and even a simple hand coping saw could be used to make the projects in this book.

- **Sew-on Velcro.** I prefer sew-on Velcro as opposed to sticky-back adhesive Velcro, which will gum up your sewing machine. Remember when sewing Velcro to projects that opposite sides of the Velcro (loop on one piece and hook on the other) must be showing in order for the Velcro to attach to itself.

- **Transfer Paper.** If you would like to transfer any of my template designs, I recommend buying a roll of graphite transfer paper. You can find it at art supply or craft stores. The graphite erases like a pencil and washes out of fabric. To use it, tear off a piece (one piece can be used over and over) and place it face down on your fabric, wood, or paper, then lay the template over it and trace over the template with a pen or anything pointed.

    When using graphite transfer paper with fabric, you'll need to trace with something that's not too sharp, so it doesn't poke through the paper and onto the fabric. You can use the back of a plastic paintbrush, or even a pen lid. The tracing tool just needs to press the graphite into the fabric; it doesn't need to draw.

- **Wire.** I love making things from wire. It's inexpensive and very satisfying. I prefer steel wire, usually 18 to 24 gauge (18 is thicker, 24 is thinner). You can buy rolls of wire at hardware stores or most craft stores. Another favorite wire I've been using is floral wire, either cloth wrapped or plain. Packs are available at craft stores. Sometimes I use steel welding rod, a very sturdy and inexpensive option. Look for it at a welding supply store. I often use ER 308L as it's not too thick, which makes the rod fairly easy to bend. Keep in mind that it's important to wear safety glasses when bending wire.

- **Woodburner.** I've had a woodburner since I was nine years old. It's a nice, non-toxic way to decorate wood toys. You can purchase a woodburner at most hardware or craft stores. Just be careful, because woodburners get very hot!

play zoo!

portable zoo animals

This portable zoo has been my son's favorite restaurant toy for over a year. He loves animals, and these folded paper versions are fun to stand up and arrange on the table. Also, they fold flat and store nicely in a mint tin.

materials

Paper (A sturdy paper works best, but any paper will do.)
Pen
Scissors
Templates (see page 192)

1. Draw the outlines for your animals using the templates or your own designs. (See page 12 on how to transfer the templates.) My animals are 2" to 4" in size, but you could make them any size you like.
2. Cut out each animal.

3. Draw designs on the animals, again following the templates or coming up with your own designs.
4. Gently fold the animals in half to stand them up.

1.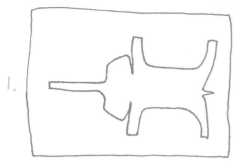

2.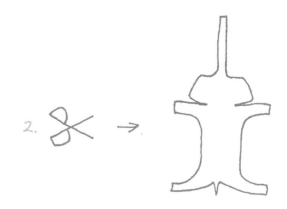

3.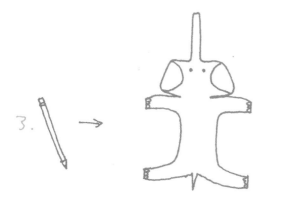

4.

zoo blanket

My kids love animals. One of their favorite activities is arranging all of their animal toys and building a zoo. So I thought it would be nice to design a simple play blanket with some shapes and colors where we could put the different animals. Blue water, green farm fields, and so on. The kids have had a lot of fun interacting with it and designing their own zoo arrangements.

Note: Keep in mind that you can make this blanket using any colors and shapes you'd like.

materials

Fabric for the background: two pieces 29" x 42" (I used a soft cotton canvas.)

Fabric for the details: various scraps of small, colorful fabrics in different shapes (I used the following):

- Red fabric: one piece, 8" x 10"
- Red fabric: one half circle, 15½" x 8½"
- Blue fabric: one piece, 17" x 13½"
- Yellow fabric: three circles, 5½" in diameter
- Black felt: one piece, 17½" x 2¾"
- Green fabric: three strips, 15½" x 2½"
- Cream colored faux fur: one circle, 8½" in diameter

Scissors and/or rotary cutter

Iron

Double-sided fusible interfacing (enough to back each piece of colored fabric, except for the faux fur)

Sewing machine

Thread (I used a cream colored thread for all of the blanket, except the "ZOO" lettering, for which I used a dark brown thread.)

1. Cut out two pieces of background fabric. You can fold a large piece of fabric and cut both pieces out at the same time. I used a rotary cutter and a metal yardstick for a straight edge guide.

2. Cut out all of the color shapes so they can be arranged on the blanket before you sew them down.

3. For the rectangular shapes (except the felt), turn under the edges ½", and sew the edges down.

4. Now arrange all the pieces on one of the large background rectangles. (See the illustration for the layout I used. Keep in mind that you need an additional ½" of the background fabric around the edges for the seam allowance.) Once the pieces are arranged to your liking, mark their positions on the background fabric using a vanishing fabric pen or chalk, then take the pieces off the blanket and set them aside.

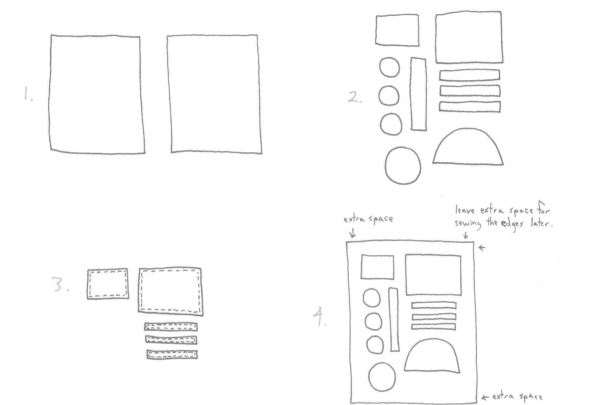

1.

2.

3.

4.

extra space

leave extra space for
sewing the edges later.

extra space

5. Following the manufacturer's directions, attach each piece of fabric, except the faux fur, to the background fabric with fusible interfacing. The fusible interfacing keeps the middle of the fabric pieces from pooching out, and it also makes sewing much easier because the pieces are already firmly in place.

For the rectangular pieces that have been hemmed, sew around all four sides to secure them in place. For the unhemmed pieces, sew them to the background fabric using a zigzag stitch to prevent the fabric from fraying. As you sew the pieces on, add any detail stitching you'd like. On my blanket, I sewed some curving lines to represent watery waves on the blue rectangle. Some arched lines on the red half circle turned this piece into the entrance gate for the zoo.

Finally, pin the faux fur circle in place, then sew around the edge using a zigzag stitch.

I did not use the fusible interfacing on this piece because the hot iron would melt the faux fur.

If you like, give your zoo a name. I drew out the letters "ZOO" with a vanishing fabric pen, then used a dark brown thread and a very small zigzag to stitch the word.

6. Now that all of the pieces are attached, place the second piece of background fabric on top of the sewn-on shapes with the right sides of the fabrics together. Pin the background pieces in place.

7. Sew around three sides of the blanket, ½" from the edge, leaving only the top edge open. Make sure you don't sew over any of the colored shapes.

8. Turn the whole blanket right side out, and iron it flat (avoiding the faux fur).

9. Now close the top by sewing a zigzag stitch all the way across the edge. Done!

5.

6.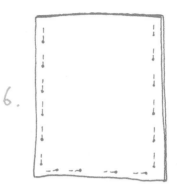

7.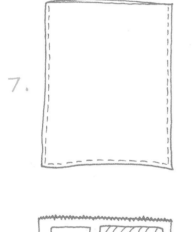

8.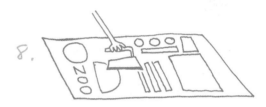

9.

animal finger puppets

Animating a finger puppet is a great way to exercise those fine motor skills without even realizing it. My children like to choose which color paper to use for each animal, and as they get older, they've become more involved in the drawing process as well. I always love hearing the stories they tell through the characters.

materials

Paper (I used colored construction paper.)
Pens or crayons
Tape or glue (I used double-sided clear tape.)
Templates (see page 193)

1. Get your paper, and draw the outlines for your animals following the templates or your own designs. (See page 12 on how to transfer the templates.) My puppets are all about 2½" wide. Cut out the finger puppets with scissors.

2. Decorate your finger puppet with a pen or crayons.

3. Use double-sided clear tape or glue to stick the ends together.

1.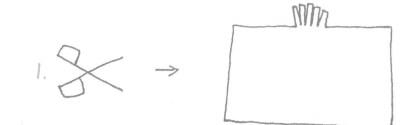

2.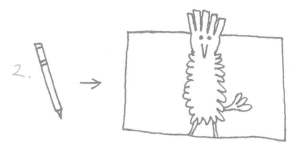

3.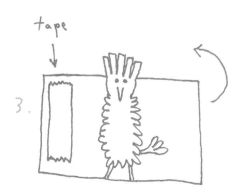

tape

small wooden animals

When my kids got to the point that they weren't interested in putting everything in their mouths, they became fascinated with very small toys. I made these wooden animals small enough to fit inside a plastic egg so we could hide them for Easter. Months later, the kids were still carrying them around, building little jungles in the house and in the yard. These treasured animals have accompanied us on many walks, snugly stowed in a pocket or hand.

materials

Wood scraps (I used ¼" plywood.)
Saw (I used a scroll saw, but a hand coping saw
    will also work.)
Sandpaper
Paint or woodburner
Beeswax polish
Templates (see page 194)

1. Draw the animal shapes on the wood following the templates or your own designs. (See page 12 on how to transfer the templates.) My animals are about 1½" in size, but you can make them any size you like. Cut them out with a saw.

2. Sand each animal to remove any splinters and rough edges.

3. Paint or woodburn a design on each animal.

4. Rub your wooden animals with some beeswax polish to protect them.

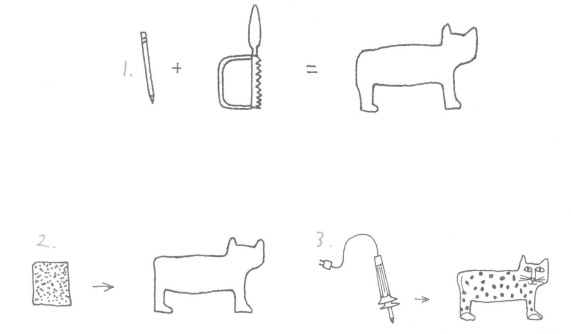

wooden spool birds

These little birds are really fun to make. The cloth stem wire is so easy to bend, you can just use your fingers. And you can create many different variations of birds: tall, short, big feathers, small feathers. In no time, you'll have your own little flock!

Note: Remember that it's always a good idea to wear safety glasses when bending wire.

materials

Wooden spool (as in a thread spool)

Wire (I recommend using 18"-long, 22-gauge cloth stem wire, which you can find in the floral section of craft stores. You can also use 12" pipe cleaner or craft wire.)

Paper (I used paper from recycled magazine covers, but any paper will work.)

Feathers (You can get feathers at craft stores, or you can even make them out of paper.)

Pen

Tape or glue (I used regular and double-sided clear tape.)

Scissors or craft knife

1. Take your 18" piece of wire. Hold the spool against the middle of the wire, and wrap the wire around the spool a couple of times. Try to keep the wire snug. (If you're using 12" pipe cleaner, then just wrap the spool once.) Twist the ends of the wire together a couple of times to secure it to the spool.

2. Bend each end of the wire into feet, and trim any excess wire with an old pair of scissors or a wire cutter. Slide the spool a little forward or backward through the wire loops to better balance the bird so it stands freely.

3. Place the end of the spool on the paper, and trace around the circle. Then, 1" above that circle, draw a smaller circle for the head. Connect the two circles to form a neck. Add some pointy head feathers if you'd like. Then cut the shape out with scissors or a craft knife.

4. Use a pen to draw eyes and a beak, and additional designs if you'd like.

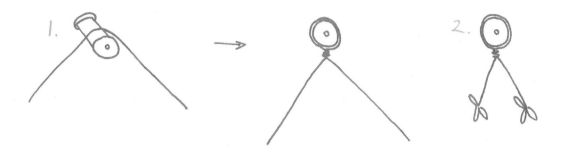

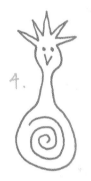

1.

2.

3.

4.

5. Attach the paper piece to the end of the spool using double-sided clear tape or glue.
6. Finally, tape the stems of the feathers to the back of the spool using clear tape. If the feathers are too long, clip them shorter and trim the feather plumes off the last ½" so you have a stem to tape to the spool.
7. Enjoy your new feathery friend!

5.

6.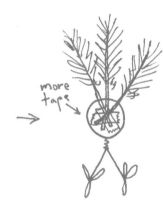

tape →

more tape →

7.

play house!

scrap wood dollhouse

Even two pieces of scrap wood can create a great imaginative space to decorate with dollhouse furniture. Use whatever size boards you can find and just nail them together!

materials

Wood: two pieces in sizes of your choosing (My
   base board was about 7" x 9", and my wall
   board was 8" x 9".)
Sandpaper
A couple of nails or screws
Beeswax polish

1. Attach the wall board to the base board with
   screws or nails.
2. Sand until smooth.

3. Rub on some beeswax polish if you'd like.
   Decorate with some Modern Dollhouse
   Furniture (see page 51).

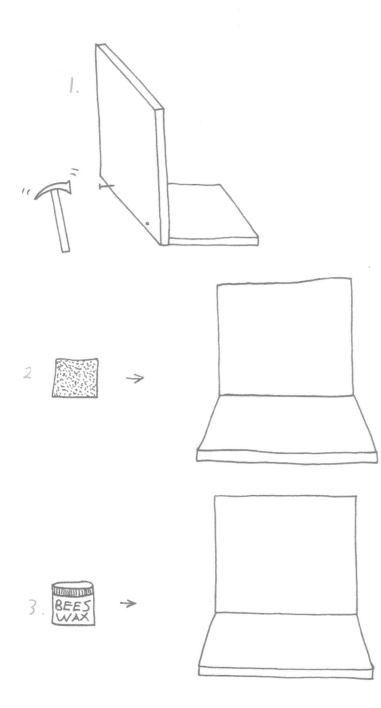

1.

2

3. BEES WAX

modern dollhouse

Playing with dollhouses is such an enjoyable and creative way to enter into another world. This simple dollhouse design provides access from all sides, giving an open, soothing, imaginative space in which to create.

materials

Wooden board: one piece about 8" long x 9" wide x ¾" thick (I used solid poplar.)

Saw (I used a skill saw for everything except step 5, where I used a jigsaw.)

Finishing nails

Nail punch and wood putty (optional, so nail heads don't show)

Beeswax polish

¼" dowel: two pieces 1" long (optional, for attaching top floor)

1. Take your board, and cut off a 28½" piece for the base of the dollhouse.
2. From the same board, cut a 20" piece for the second level of the dollhouse.
3. Now cut three pieces that are 8½" each. These pieces will form the three walls on the base floor.
4. Take one of the 8½" pieces from step 3, and cut 3½" off one side so you end up with a 3½" by 8½" piece.
5. Take another 8½" piece from step 3, and cut a doorway to make the opening to the patio. I used a jigsaw to cut my doorway, which is 5½" wide by 7" tall. Cutting an opening like this one is sometimes tricky. Just keep in mind that it doesn't need to be perfect.

Alternatively, you could just leave the wood intact and have a closed, separate patio.

6. Take the last 8½" piece from step 3, and stand it up at the end of the floor piece from step 1. Then take the patio wall from step 5, and stand it on edge near the opposite end of the floor. Gently place the second level (from step 2) on top, and nail the roof to the two walls.
7. Flip over the dollhouse, and nail the two walls to the floor.
8. Insert the 3½"-wide wall between the two walls to create two rooms, and nail the wall in place from the top and bottom. I put my wall slightly off center so the two rooms on the main floor are slightly different sizes. The smaller room is 8" long, and the larger one is about 9½".

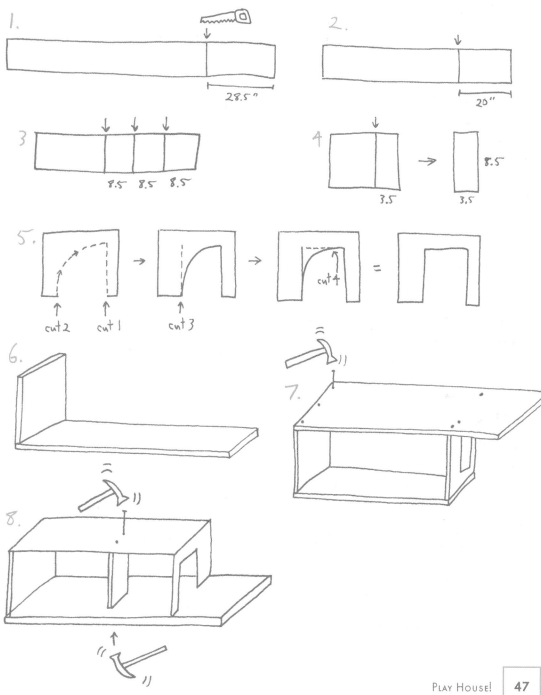

1.

28.5"

2.

20"

3.

8.5   8.5   8.5

4.

3.5   3.5   8.5

5.

cut 2   cut 1   cut 3   cut 4   =

6.

7.

8.

9. Go back to your original board, and cut a piece 6½" long. Then cut it in half widthwise. These two pieces will create the walls on the top floor.

10. Cut an 11" by 5½" piece from the original board to form the roof on the top floor. (See the illustration; this step will require two cuts).

11. Gently place the top floor roof from step 10 on the two walls from step 9, and nail the roof to the walls. Line up the walls so they are flush on the back side and allow an overhang on the front and right side. (See the top view illustration.)

12. Attach the top floor to the bottom floor. This step can be done two different ways. Because the outside edge wall is flush with the lower level wall, it can't be easily nailed. The first method is to slide the top floor over a little so you can easily nail both walls from the bottom. If you want the outside wall to be flush, another option is to diagonally tack nails from the sides. The second method, which I suggest, is to drill two holes in the outside wall of the top floor and corresponding holes in the roof of the bottom floor. Then attach the pieces by inserting and gluing a ¼" dowel in each hole. It's easier than you think, and the results are sturdy and beautiful. Finally, nail the second wall in place from the bottom.

13. With the remaining wood create a 1"-tall fence around the patio. To do this, measure the lengths you will need so it will fit as well as possible. Then nail the lengths to the patio from the bottom. I used two fence pieces that were 8½" long and one that was 7¾" long.

14. Get some sandpaper, and sand everything smooth. If you choose to hide the nail heads, use a nail punch to pound the nails farther into the wood and then cover them with wood putty. When the putty is dry, sand it smooth. Finally, rub some beeswax polish over the whole house to protect the wood and give it a nice finish.

15. Done! For ideas on Modern Dollhouse Furniture, see page 51.

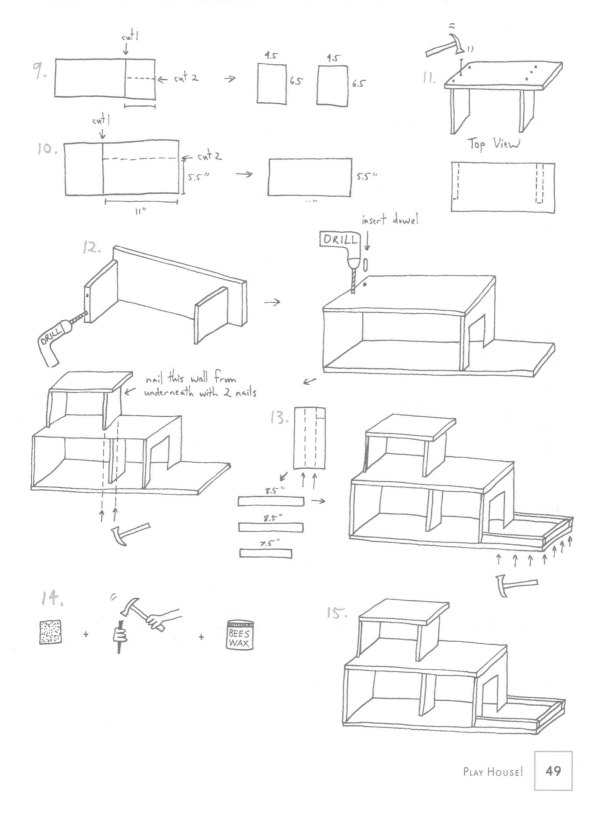

9.

cut 1

← cut 2

→

4.5
6.5

4.5
6.5

11.

Top View

10.

cut 1

← cut 2

5.5"

11"

→

5.5"

12.

DRILL

insert dowel

DRILL

→

nail this wall from underneath with 2 nails

13.

8.5"

8.5"

7.5"

→

14.

+

+

BEES WAX

15.

modern dollhouse furniture

Modern dollhouse furniture is just like real modern furniture: the simpler, the better. My kids and I also love to collect objects from nature, such as pinecones, rocks, and cut branches, and bring them into the dollhouse. Kids really enjoy collecting and gathering. Even a year after I built the dollhouse, my son still spots a perfect rock or twig while we're on walks and bicycle rides and says, "This will be good for the dollhouse!"

Note on building the furniture: The wood furniture designs here are extremely simple and fast to make. They usually involve only one or two pieces of scrap wood just glued together. You can find scrap hardwood sold online for very little money, or you can visit a local wood shop or woodworking shop and ask for wood scraps. Woodworkers hate to waste wood and will be happy to give their scraps to you. As for the bent-wire furniture, wire is very inexpensive and can be bought at hardware or craft stores. Creating furniture out of wire might seem more intimidating, but once you start bending, you will see how fun it is. Just don't be bothered if your creations are not perfect or if you have to start over with a new piece of wire. As always, it's a good idea to wear eye protection while working with wire.

materials

Scrap wood (hardwood rather than plywood)

Saw (hand coping saw or electric scroll saw)

Wood glue

Sandpaper

Fabric scraps

Scissors and/or rotary cutter

Sewing machine or needle and thread

Hot glue gun (optional, for upholstering chairs and
benches)

Wire (I used a 20-gauge steel wire because it's
very easy to bend.)

Needle-nose pliers, for bending wire

Small file or emery board (used for fingernails),
to file the ends of sharp wires

Beeswax polish

Objects from nature (small pinecones, rocks, twigs,
and so on)

RUGS

Rugs are the easiest things to make, and they are often the subtle additions that really make a dollhouse come to life. I cut my rugs out of scrap fabric, and that's it. If you have faux fur, cut it outside so you don't get fur everywhere, then shake it out to get rid of all the loose fur. For other rugs, I used a natural canvas fabric. I cut the rug shape, then pulled off a few of the strings on the edge to make a fringed look. Another option is to sew a design on a rug to create a line pattern or an image.

Tree Pots

Trees are another great thing to place in a doll-house. The easiest way to make a pot for a tree is to cut a round circle from a piece of wood, sand it, and drill a small hole in the middle. Rub a little beeswax polish on if you'd like, then find a twig outside and stick it in the drilled hole.

Another option is to make a tree pot from wire. To do this, start by winding the wire into a small cylinder. This will be the hole for the twig in the center of the pot. When you get to the bottom of the cylinder, gradually wind the wire in larger circles to create the base of the pot. Then start winding circles upward to create the sides of the pot. When you are finished, insert a twig, then fill the remaining space with tiny rocks for a pleasing appearance and additional weight.

Wood Benches

One of my benches is just a block of wood scrap, 2¼" long, about ½" tall, and 1" wide. I sanded it and polished it with beeswax. Then I took two very small fabric scraps, folded them, and placed them on the bench to look like blankets. You can also cut magazine covers into tiny pretend magazines.

I made another bench from a rectangular scrap of wood, roughly 2" long. Then I cut a small piece of wood the same length, and glued it on for a low backrest. After applying the glue, I clamped the pieces overnight while the glue dried. To finish the bench, I applied some beeswax polish. Then I added an upholstered seat cushion by cutting a piece of thin cardboard, wrapping it with a fabric scrap, and hot gluing it to the bench.

Wood Bed

The wood bed is made almost just like the upholstered wood bench. I used a rectangular wood piece, roughly 3" long. Then I cut a small piece of wood for the headboard, glued it on, and applied beeswax. To create a blanket, I turned under the edges of a piece of scrap fabric and sewed around them quickly with the sewing machine. I just placed it on the bed. The kids like taking the blanket on and off.

Side Table

I made a small side table using one of the little pieces of wood that you sometimes get in the packaging with Plan Toys. I'd been saving them, and finally found a good use for them. The piece of wood is about 1½" wide by 3" long. I just made a few cuts and glued it together.

Wire Chairs

When making these wire chairs, you can try to follow my instructions, but it might be best to take my basic idea for the shape and design, and just dive in and start bending. If something doesn't seem sturdy, then wrap the wire around until it feels solid. If you lose faith halfway through, keep going. These things have a way of pulling themselves together at the last minute. And if your attempt doesn't work, don't worry; it only takes a few minutes to try another one.

For the upright chair, I started with the lower back of the seat and then made the seat frame and legs. Then I made the frame for the backrest and wrapped it with wire two or three times to reinforce it. Last, I made an additional wire frame over the seat to slide the seat cushion onto. When you are finished, tuck the ends of the wire into the chair so they don't poke out anywhere. If an end is sharp, you can file it with a small file or a rough emery board to make it smooth and safe. For the seat

cushion, I cut a piece of thin cardboard, wrapped it with scrap fabric, and glued the fabric to the cardboard with a hot glue gun. I left one side of the fabric open and unglued so I could slide the cushion onto that additional wire frame over the seat.

For the lounge chair, I started with the frame outline and legs. I left the back legs extra long so I could attach brown buttons for the wheels. After the frame and legs were done, I wrapped wire around and around, all down the length of the chair. Finally, I attached the buttons by bending the wire through the buttonholes. I must admit that was the tricky part. If it's not working for you, just bend the legs in half and leave them without wheels.

paper barn and animals

When I was a kid, I lived next to my grandparents' small farm where I got to feed the animals and ride the horses. Now that I live in the city, I have to make my own little farm out of paper. It sure is a lot less work than a real farm! I borrowed a tree from the dollhouse (see page 53) for some extra scenery.

materials

Paper (I used a sturdy paper, then painted it. But
    you could use any kind of paper you'd like.)
Scissors or craft knife
Glue or glue stick
Templates (see pages 195-96)

BARN

1. Following the template, draw the shape of
   the barn on your paper and cut it out. (See
   page 12 on how to transfer the templates.)
   Fold in the sides across the dotted lines.
   When flat, my barn was 14" by 8½", but you
   can make it whatever size you'd like.

2. Fold the roof down, lining up the bent
   walls so they are flush at the front edge. Use
   double-sided tape to secure the wall flaps to
   each other on each side.

Barn

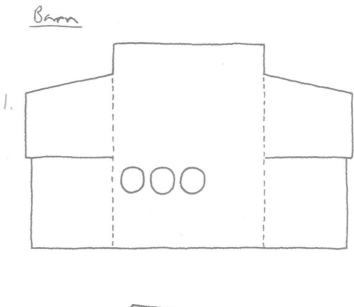

1.

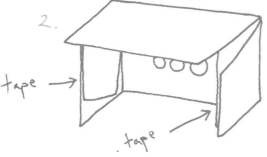

2.

tape →

tape →

Animals

1. Fold your paper in half to make the animals extra sturdy. Draw the animals following the templates or your own designs so that the bottom of the feet line up against the fold of the paper and the two sides will be joined at the feet . (See page 12 on how to transfer the templates.) Cut them out.

2. Glue the sides of the animals together to create sturdy and flat paper animals. (I prefer a glue stick for this step.)

3. Cut out the shapes of the foot stands, and slide them into the leg notches to make the animals stand up.

Animals

1.

2.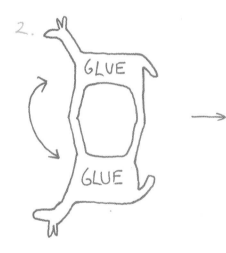

GLUE

GLUE

3.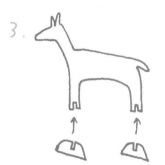

embroidered pillow doll

There is something special about hand embroidery—it's so easy to see the care that goes into it, and the results are beautiful. This simple Embroidered Pillow Doll can provide a child with an imaginative companion for playtime and naptime. It's been a year and a half, and my daughter still sleeps with her pillow doll.

materials

Fabric: two pieces about 10" x 7", or to fit your embroidery hoop (I used a natural, coarse weave cotton.)

Embroidery hoop (I used an oval 5" x 9" hoop.)

Embroidery thread and needle (I used black thread.)

Scissors and/or rotary cutter

Sewing machine, or needle and thread

Stuffing

Template (see page 197)

1. Draw the doll design on the fabric using the template or your own design. (See page 12 on how to transfer the templates.)

2. Put the drawn-on fabric in the embroidery hoop.

3. Prepare your thread for embroidery. I usually cut my thread into 2' lengths so it's manageable. Embroidery thread has six strands. For this doll, I pulled the thread apart to vary the thicknesses of the line. If you would like a consistent line width, I suggest using three strands of thread. (To see where I used different thicknesses, refer to the template.)

   Embroider along your drawn lines using a backstitch (see the illustration).

4. Once the embroidery is complete, cut the fabric down to 7½" by 5", then cut a rounded top. Be sure that your embroidery is centered on the fabric and that you have at least a ½" seam allowance around the embroidery.

5. Take the second piece of fabric for the back of the doll, and cut it into the same shape as the front.

6. Layer the pieces of fabric, right sides together.

7. With a machine or by hand, sew around the sides and top of the doll, about ½" from the edge.

8. Turn the doll right side out, and fill it with stuffing.

9. Fold under the bottom edge ½", and machine or hand sew the bottom closed.

1.

2.

separate threads   Backstitch

3.

4.

5. +

6. ← back of embroidery

7.

8.

9.

small wire dolls

These wire dolls provide a great way for children to use their imagination and creative design sense. They're engaging to play with and fun to make. You might need to bend the wire, but the child will love looking at small scraps of fabric and overseeing the designs for the clothing.

Note: Remember that it's always a good idea to wear safety glasses when bending wire.

materials

Wire (I used a 22-gauge wire that's thin enough to
do most of the bending with my fingers. I used
pliers when wrapping the ends or making a
tight angle.)

Needle-nose pliers and wire cutter (usually built
into the pliers)

File or coarse emery board, to sand pointy wires
smooth

Fabric scraps, to make clothes

Scissors and/or rotary cutter

Sewing machine, or needle and thread

Hot glue gun (optional, for clothes)

Dress

1. Start out with a piece of fabric approximately 4" by 4". Fold the fabric in half, and cut
out a simple dress shape.
2. Fold under the bottom edge ¼", and sew.

3. Now fold dress in half, right sides together,
lining up the side edges. Then sew along the
side about ¼" from the edge.
4. Turn the dress right-side out.

Dress

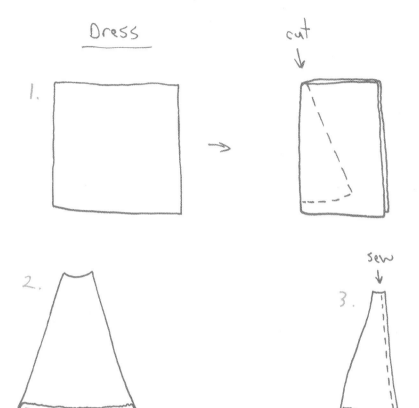

1.

cut →

2.

3. sew

4.

Hat

Note: The hat is best fitted to a finished doll head.

1. Bend the head of the doll to create a small rectangle on top to hold the hat.
2. Take two pieces of felt. Cut out a simple hat shape, making sure the main part of the hat is bigger than the rectangle on the head (while also keeping the seam allowance in mind). Sew around the edges, leaving an opening at the bottom.
3. Now slide the hat onto the head.

Pants, Scarf, and Tie

Make a simple pair of pants, a scarf, and a tie from scraps of fabric. Simply cut out the basic shapes in the size you think will work for your doll. For the pants and tie, include tabs that you can easily fold over the wire doll. To attach, either tie or hot glue the pieces together so they stay on the doll. (See the illustrations in step 3 of Wire Dolls.)

Wire Dolls

1. Start with about 20″ of wire to make a 4″- to 5″-tall doll. At one end of the wire, make a circle for the base. Close off the circle by wrapping one end of the wire around the circle a couple times.
2. Bend the wire flat against the bottom through the middle of the circle, then bend it straight up at the middle to make the torso of the figure.
3. The torso of each doll has slightly different bends to hold the different types of clothing.

   For the doll with the dress: Keep the wire straight all the way up the torso. At the neck of the figure, bend another little circle to hold up the dress. Then slide the dress down over the wire and rest it on the small neck circle.

   For the doll with the scarf and pants: Bend a small cross bar at the hips to wrap the pants around and a small loop at the neck to support the scarf.

   For the doll with the tie and hat: Keep the wire straight all the way up the torso, then loop it down one side of the body, wrap it around the lower torso once, and loop it back up the other side, creating an oval body shape.

   Bend another circle for the head (for the doll with the hat, make a small square bend on the head for the hat), wrap the end of the wire around the neck a couple of times for strength, and then clip off the excess wire. If the wire end is pointy, file it smooth and try to tuck it under the clothing.
4. Once the doll is made, do any last little bends on the base and torso so the doll will stand up firmly.

Hat

1.

2.

3.

wire dolls

1.

2.

3.

tie on scarf

cross bar to hold up pants

fold and hot glue

bend for hat

fold and hot glue necktie

4.

wooden sleeping doll

My children love to have someone they can tuck into bed and take care of. This sleeping doll and bed are very easy to make. You can also make the bed for a favorite doll that your child might already have.

materials

Fabric: one piece, 4" x 8", for the bed; one piece,
   2" x 3½", for the blanket (I used faux fur for the
   blanket.)
Scissors and/or rotary cutter
Sewing machine
Wood: one piece 1¼" x 3½" (Mine was ¼" thick.)
Saw (hand coping saw or scroll saw)
Paint, pen, or woodburner, to draw the eyes on
   the doll
Sandpaper
Beeswax polish
Template (see page 198)

BED AND BLANKET

1. Start with the 4" by 8" piece of fabric. Fold
   over the short ends ¼" twice, and sew them in
   place.
2. Now fold over the long ends ¼" twice,
   but don't sew them yet. (You might need to pin
   them or iron them flat.)
3. Now fold over the lower end of the fabric about 1½" from the top edge. Pin the fabric
   in place, and sew all the way down each side.
4. For the blanket, cut a scrap of fabric and
   insert it into the bed. I used faux fur, but felt
   would be a good choice, too.

DOLL

1. Take a small scrap of wood, and following
   the template or your own design, draw on the
   doll shape with a pencil. (See page 12 on how
   to transfer the templates.)
2. Cut out the doll shape with a saw.
3. Sand the wood until it is smooth.
4. Woodburn or paint two curved eyelids
   on the doll, and rub beeswax polish on it if
   you'd like.
5. Now let the doll get some sleep.

Bed and Blanket

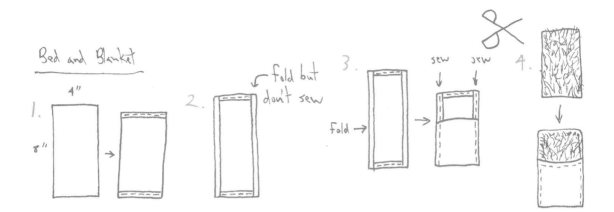

1. 4″ 8″

2. fold but don't sew

3. fold | sew sew

4.

Doll

1.

2.

3.

4.

5. z z z z

play with building toys, cars, and trucks!

slotted building discs

While reading an issue of *ArtForum* magazine, I came across a brilliant Damián Ortega sculpture made of tortillas. I immediately wished I could play with them. So I scanned some recent collage circles I'd made, printed them out, and made these building discs. They are surprisingly tricky to build with, but amazingly addicting. If you have older kids, they will definitely be challenged. My three-year-olds are having a great time with them too, but their structures are much more simple. Also, they fit perfectly into a round candy tin, which makes them very handy to take to restaurants or anywhere else on the go.

materials

Paper (A sturdy paper works best.)

Scissors

Drinking glass or something round for tracing the
circle shapes

Glue stick (optional, to glue pieces together)

Pens (optional, to decorate the circles.)

Template (optional, see page 198)

1. If your paper doesn't feel sturdy enough, glue two pieces together with a glue stick. I printed my design on stiff paper then glued some yellow construction paper to the back with a glue stick for extra strength. Use a glass or anything round to trace the circles onto your paper, or use the template. (See page 12 on how to transfer the templates.) I made 24 circles, about 2½" in diameter.

2. Cut out the circles.

3. Decorate the circles by drawing on them, or just leave them plain. You could also use decorative patterned paper.

4. Now cut four thin notches in each circle. Done!

1.

2.

3.

4.

abstract vertical puzzle

I created this toy as a way to help my children develop dexterity and creativity. For my three-year-old twins, pegging the pieces to the design wall requires just the right amount of physical challenge. And the artistic arrangements they come up with are great. This toy has been a big hit with all of the cousins and friends, and it can be made with almost any scrap wood you can find.

materials

Wood: two pieces in sizes of your choosing (My
    base board was about 9" x 9", and my wall
    board was 9" x 12".)
Wood scraps, for the various pieces
Wood dowel: ¼" diameter
Saw (I used a scroll saw to cut out the wood
    shapes and dowel pieces.)
Drill with a ⁹⁄₃₂" drill bit (which is just a little larger
    than the ¼" dowel)
Sandpaper
A couple of nails or screws
Paint
Beeswax polish

1. Get a piece of board for the base and
   another for the wall. Using a drill with a ⁹⁄₃₂" bit,
   drill a bunch of holes in the wall board. Make
   the holes about 1" apart, but don't bother measuring—just eyeball it, because it doesn't mat-
   ter if the holes are straight or evenly spaced.

2. Attach the wall board to the middle of
   the base board from below with screws or
   nails. If you use screws, you might have to
   predrill holes so you don't split the wood.

3. Cut scraps of wood into various shapes.
   I made about 12 pieces ranging in size from 3"
   by 3" to ¾" by 8". Once they're cut, drill a hole
   in each one using the same ⁹⁄₃₂" drill bit.

4. Sand the wooden base and the shapes,
   then paint the shapes as desired. After they
   dry, rub beeswax polish on them if you'd like.

5. Finally, with a saw, cut the dowel into 2" lengths.
   Make as many dowels as you have shapes.

6. Start creating some vertical designs!

1. DRILL

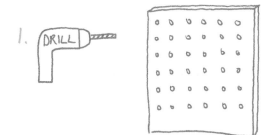

2. screw

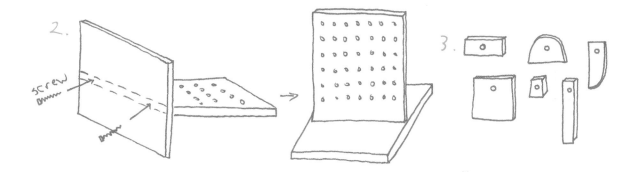

3.

4.

5.

flat block set

My kids often lay their blocks flat and create designs on the floor. I thought it would be fun to have more shapes and colors to use in their compositions, so I made this flat block set. Since the blocks are flat, they're very portable. I sewed a little bag for the blocks, so it's easy to throw them into a purse and take them on the go. They're perfect for tables at restaurants or cafés.

Note: You could also cut these shapes out of colored or painted paper for a faster, easier option.

materials

Wood (I used ¼" plywood.)
Saw (hand coping saw or scroll saw)
Sandpaper
Paint
Beeswax polish
Fabric: one piece 7½" x 17", for the carrying bag (I
    used a natural denim fabric.)
Scissors and/or rotary cutter
Sewing machine
Snap or Velcro, to close the bag

BLOCKS

1. With a pencil, draw a variety of basic shapes
   on the wood, such as circles, half circles,
   squares, rectangles, and triangles. My circular
   pieces ranged in size from 1" to 3" in diameter,
   and the long thin pieces ranged from about
   1½" to 5½" long.
2. Cut out the shapes with a saw. Don't
   worry if your lines aren't perfect. Your project
   will look more handmade that way, which is a
   good thing.
3. Sand the wooden shapes to remove any
   splinters or rough edges.
4. Paint the shapes as desired.
5. After the paint is dry, rub on some beeswax polish to protect the blocks.

BAG

1. Take your piece of fabric, and turn under the
   edges ½" on each short end. Sew the edges in
   place.
2. Embroider a design on the bag if you'd like. I
   used the machine for this. Make sure you embroider on the right side of the fabric.
3. Fold the fabric in half lengthwise, right
   sides together, and sew along the two sides
   of the bag.
4. Turn the bag right-side out.
5. Attach a snap or sew on some Velcro to
   close the bag.

Blocks

1.
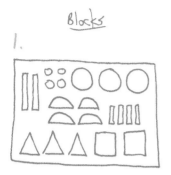

2.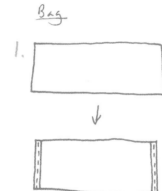

3.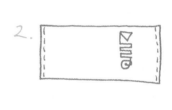

4.

5.

Bag

1.

2.

3.

4.

5.

rubber band race cars

This activity is great for budding car enthusiasts. Many fun games can be made with this rubber band race car: try to launch it through a tunnel of books or blocks, make two and race them, see whose can go the farthest, add a special paint job with paints or markers. You can hold the rubber band with your fingers, but for smaller hands, it's fun to make a little cardboard launch garage. Off to the races!

materials

Cardboard: two pieces, 3" x 7" for the car body; one piece, 6" x 1½" for the car back; and one piece, 6" x 9" for the launching garage (A stiff shoe box cardboard or corrugated cardboard works best.)

Scissors

One paper clip

Pliers, to bend the paper clip

One or two (depending on size) rubber bands

Masking tape

Paint or markers (optional)

1. Take one of the 3" by 7" cardboard pieces for the top of the car, and make a bend about 1" from the end. This will be the nose of the car.
2. Use two pieces of tape to attach the nose of the car to the other 3" by 7" piece of cardboard.
3. Take the piece of cardboard that is 6" by 1½", and bend it in thirds.
4. Insert the bent piece of cardboard into the back of the car, and tape it in place.
5. Now take some pliers, and bend up one end of the paper clip.
6. Tape the paper clip securely to the nose of the car. Make sure the bent part is sticking up toward the front of the car.
7. Take the piece of cardboard for the launching garage. From that piece of cardboard, cut out an opening 5½" by 4".
8. Cut out two notches for the rubber band about 3" up on each side of the launching garage. Insert a rubber band into the notches. If your rubber band is too small, loop two rubber bands together. The rubber band should fit snuggly in place, but it should not be so taut that it buckles the cardboard.
9. Paint or color your car if you'd like.
10. Hook the paper clip into the rubber band. Pull the car back, let it go, and watch it zoom across the floor!

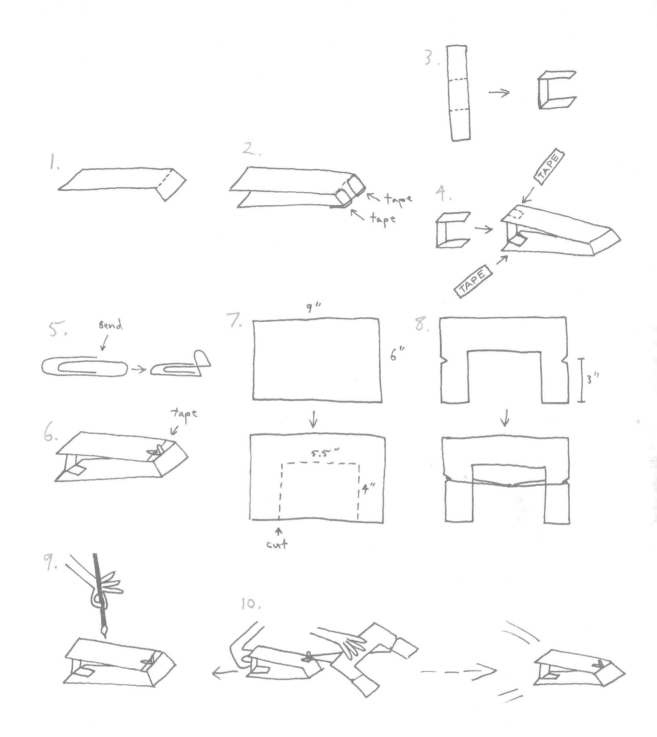

small wooden trucks

For kids who love trucks, a little portable truck stash is a great thing to have around. I made this set for my nephew and put it in a mint tin.

materials

Wood (I used ¼" plywood.)
Saw (I used a scroll saw, but a hand coping saw
    will also work.)
Sandpaper
Paint or woodburner
Beeswax polish
Templates (see page 199)

1. Following the templates or your own designs,
   draw the truck shapes on the wood and cut
   them out with a saw. (See page 12 on how to
   transfer the templates.)
2. Sand all the wooden trucks to remove
   splinters and smooth out any rough edges.
3. Paint the trucks or woodburn a design
   on them like I did.
4. Rub the trucks with some beeswax polish to
   protect the wood.
5. To make a nice little carrying container
   for your trucks, you can cut out some felt and
   glue it into a mint tin.

1.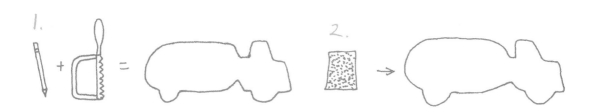

2.

3.

4.

5.

wooden nature scene

Wooden slot scenes are a great way for kids to build an imaginative world; young children especially love the satisfaction of being able to fit the pieces into the slots and make them stand up. You can also use the small wooden animals (see page 29) and the wooden trucks (see page 95) to create more diverse scenarios.

materials

Wood scraps: ¼" plywood, for the shapes and figures

Wood: one piece, 3" x 9½" x ½", for the base (I used pine.); three strips, ¾" x 9½" x ½", to create the slots (Each strip of wood should be as long as your base.)

Saw (I used a skill saw for the base and a scroll saw for the shapes and figures.)

Finishing nails

Paint

Beeswax polish

Templates (see page 200)

1. First create the base. Using a saw, cut the wood to the measurement above. You can make this toy however big or small as you'd like, so use whatever wood is most convenient. Then sand it smooth.

2. Take the three strips of wood, and cut them to the length of the base.

3. Nail one of the wood strips to the top of the base along the edge.

4. Set the ¼" plywood that you'll use for the shapes and figures on its edge next to the nailed-down strip. Arrange the second strip so that the ¼" plywood will snuggly fit between the two strips but easily slide in and out of the gap. Once the fit is good, then nail the second strip down. Repeat this step for the final strip.

5. Now draw some shapes on the plywood using the templates or your own designs, and cut them out. (See page 12 on how to transfer the templates.) Leave a little extra wood at the bottom of your designs so they can be comfortably propped up inside the slots. (My trees measured 3" to 4" tall and my mountains 2½" to 4½" tall.)

6. Sand all the pieces smooth, and paint them. After they dry, rub beeswax polish on them if you'd like.

1.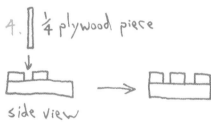

2.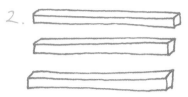

3.

4.  ¼ plywood piece

side view

5.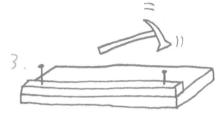

6.

play music!

sewn trumpet

This trumpet is a sweet companion for budding musicians. With the stitching and design, it asks to be picked up. And the feel of the buttons on the mouth and fingertips make it pleasing to play. I used a sturdy canvas material for the body and red cotton for the accent color. For the valves and mouthpiece, I chose colorful vintage buttons that looked fun and had a good feel.

materials

Fabric: two pieces, 10" x 18" for body; two pieces,
    4" x 5" for the color accent
Four buttons, for the valves and mouthpiece
Stuffing
Scissors and/or rotary cutter
Sewing machine
Embroidery thread (optional, for sewing on the
    buttons)
Template (see page 201)

1. Draw the trumpet shape on one piece of fabric following the template or your own design. (See page 12 on how to transfer the templates.)

2. Stack the two layers of material, and cut out the two main body pieces along the lines you've drawn. I used a rotary cutter to cut out both pieces at once.

3. Cut two oval shapes measuring 3" by 4½" from the accent material.

4. Pin one accent oval to one of the body pieces, and zigzag stitch it in place using a dark or contrasting thread. Do the same thing with the second oval and body piece. Make sure to pin and sew the second contrast piece to the side that's opposite the first, so both ovals will be facing out at the end.

5. Set the sewing machine to a straight stitch, and using the same dark thread, sew the lines for the valves, bell, and mouthpiece on each body piece.

6. Stack the two body pieces on top of each other, right sides together (the red accent ovals will be inside). Pin the pieces together, and sew only along the top of the trumpet and down the mouthpiece area, about ¼" from the edge.

1.

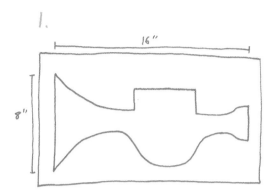

16"

8"

2.

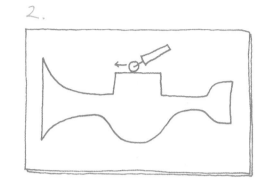

3.

4.

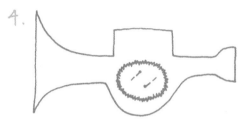

5.

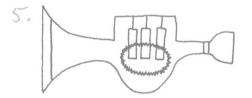

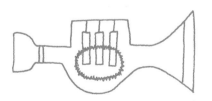

6.

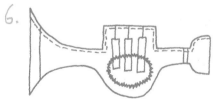

7. Turn the trumpet right-side out. Using a thread that matches your fabric and with a zigzag stitch, sew together half of the bottom edge, from the mouthpiece to the beginning of the bell.

8. Stuff the top half of the trumpet with stuffing.

9. Finish sewing the bottom of the trumpet with more zigzag stitches, leaving the bell end open.

10. Pack in more stuffing through the open bell end, then zigzag stitch the edge of the bell so the trumpet is fully closed.

11. Hand sew the buttons on the trumpet with embroidery thread, and tie a sturdy knot under each button.

12. Turn on some Miles Davis or Louis Armstrong, and play along!

7.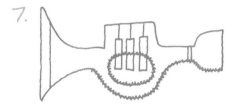

8.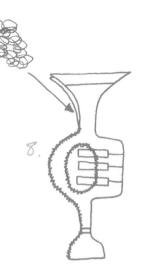

9.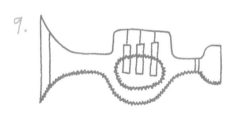

10.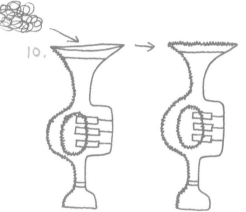

11.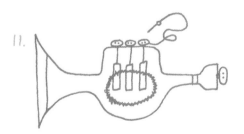

hand-drawn fabric instruments

These fabric instruments are a great way to interact with music. Dance around while listening to your favorite songs or blast out songs of your own. They're also soft enough for a cozy nap.

materials

Fabric: two pieces, approximately 12" x 19" (I used
   a natural denim and drew on the back side,
   which is smoother.)
Stuffing
Fabric pens
Hair dryer, for drying the pen ink
Scissors and/or rotary cutter
Sewing machine
Templates (see page 202)

Note: All of these instruments are made the
   same way.

1. Cut two pieces of material to the size and
   shape you want. (See the templates for the
   dimensions of my instruments.)
2. With a fabric pen, draw an instrument
   design on the fabric following the templates
   or your own designs. (See page 12 on how to
   transfer the templates.) For this part, if your
   child is old enough, you could let them do the
   drawing. The pens I use are non-toxic, but
   they are still very hard to wash off clothes,
   so beware. Another option is to let the child
   make an instrument drawing on a piece of
   paper with regular pens or crayons, and then
   use their drawing as a template for the fabric
   instrument you make.
3. After the drawing is finished, blow
   the pen ink with a hot hair dryer to set the ink.
   Once this is done, the ink is permanent and
   will withstand the washing machine.
4. Put the two cut fabric shapes right sides
   together (with your drawing on the inside), and
   sew around the edges, leaving a few inches unsewn so you can turn the shape right-side out.
5. Turn the fabric right-side out, and fill it
   with stuffing.
6. Sew the opening shut. Done!

1.

2.

3.

4. ← leave opening

5.

6.

wooden bead drum

The Wooden Bead Drum is another instrument that's fun to play and easy to make. Kids love poking the strings through the holes on the drum and threading the beads. And when it's finished, this drum makes a satisfying percussion sound yet maintains a reasonable decibel level. Nice!

materials

Wood (I used one 8" x 5" piece of ¼" plywood.)
String
Wooden beads
Saw (hand coping saw or scroll saw)
Drill
Sandpaper
Scissors
Paint
Beeswax polish

1. Draw the drum shape on the wood. Use a saw to cut out the shape for the whole drum.
2. Drill eight holes along the sides, about ½" from the edge. The strings will go through each hole.
3. Sand the wood until it is smooth.
4. Paint the drum if you'd like, and cover it with beeswax when the paint is dry.
5. Cut eight pieces of string, about 8" in length.
6. Tie knots in the ends of each string, and then string them through the holes in the drum.
7. Slide a bead onto a piece of string. Leaving about 1" of string between the bead and drum, tie a knot to secure the bead. Snip off the ends of the string with scissors. Repeat this step with each string.

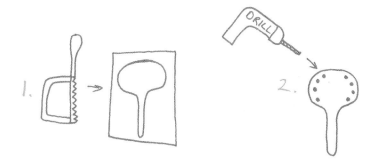

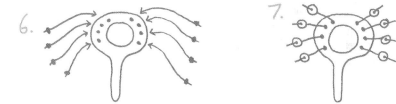

bottle cap tambourine

This bottle cap tambourine will get you shaking and moving to the beat with its moveable parts and interesting sound. My daughter was shaking and dancing so fast I could hardly snap a photo. Awesome!

materials

Wood: one stick, ¾" thick and about 14" long,
   for the handle; and one thin strip, ¾" thick and
   about 7" long, for the top.
Five nails: My nails were 1¼" long.
Nine bottle caps
Drill (optional)
Saw (hand coping saw or scroll saw)
Sandpaper
Paint
Beeswax polish

1. Take the nine bottle caps, and pound them flat
   with a hammer.
2. Make a hole in the center of each bottle
   cap, either with a drill or by pounding a nail
   through them. Make sure the holes are bigger
   than the nails you'll be using for the finished
   tambourine so the caps will be able to freely
   jingle up and down.
3. Take the long piece of wood for the
   handle, and cut off two small squares for the
   middle pieces of the tambourine. Use the
   remaining long piece for the handle.
4. Use the 7"-long (or about half as long as
   your handle) and ¾"-wide (or same width as
   the wood for the handle) piece for the top. I
   used a thin scrap of plywood. Then drill five

small holes in the smaller piece of wood for
the nails to go through. Make sure the holes
are spaced so all three stacks of bottle caps
have room to move freely.

5. Before assembling the tambourine, sand
   all the wood pieces until they are smooth and
   paint them if you'd like.
6. Hold the wood pieces in place, and
   pound a nail in each end of the chamber.
7. Poke a nail through one of the three middle
   holes, then stack three bottle caps on the nail.
   Pound the nail into the wood handle. Repeat this
   step with the other two stacks of bottle caps.
8. Rub the wood with beeswax polish if you'd like.
9. Shaky, shaky, clap, shaky, shaky, shaky,
   clap, shaky, shaky, shaky, clap!

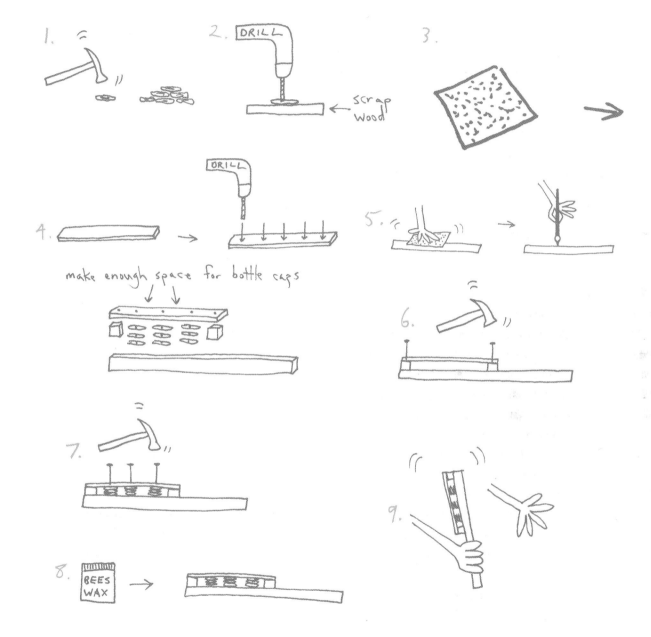

1.

2. DRILL

← Scrap Wood

3.

4. → DRILL

make enough space for bottle caps

5.

6.

7.

8. BEES WAX →

9.

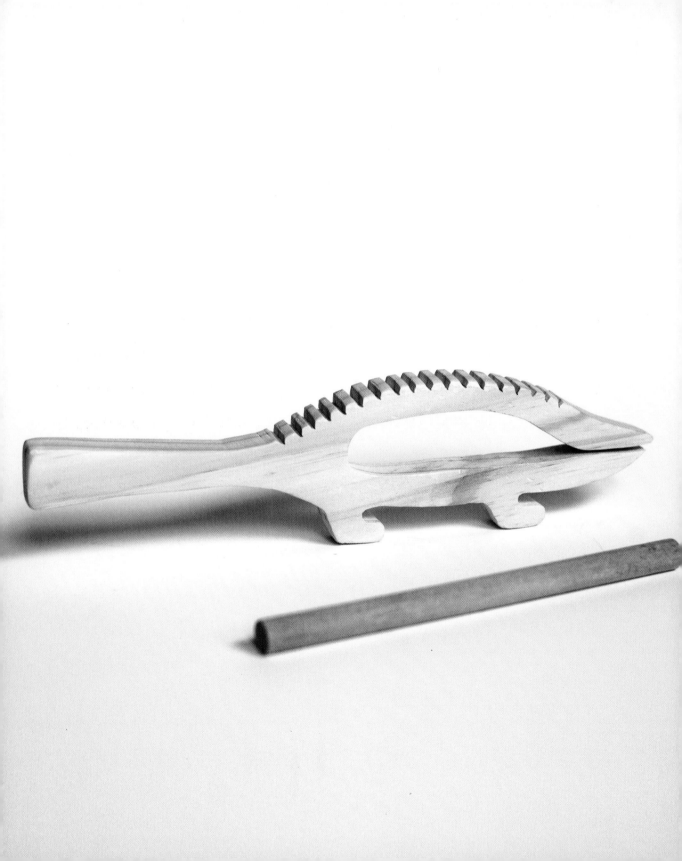

wooden guiro

Try this easy way to make a Wooden Guiro, a great percussion instrument that's really fun to play. Make music by sliding the stick back and forth over the serrated surface or by tapping the top like a wood block. You can find some great rhythm examples if you search for guiro videos or music online.

materials

Wood: one piece, 10" x 3" x ¾", for the instrument
   (I used pine.)
Wood dowel: ½" diameter x 7" long, for the stick
Saw (hand coping saw or scroll saw)
Sandpaper
Beeswax polish
Template (see page 203)

1. Take the block of wood, and draw the shape for the guiro following the template or your own design. (See page 12 on how to transfer the templates.) I made mine in the shape of an animal, but you could make a simpler version. Cut out the shape with a saw.

2. With the basic shape cut out, make another cut to hollow out the middle a little. This gives the instrument a louder sound.

3. Next, use the saw to cut out notches on the top. Make the grooves about ¼" apart. If you make them too close together, the wood points will chip off over time.

4. Sand any rough edges, and apply beeswax polish if you'd like.

5. Use a dowel stick or the handle of a wooden spoon, and play!

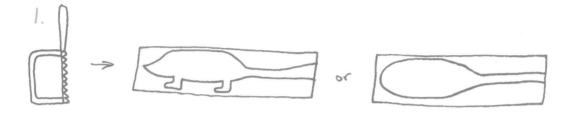

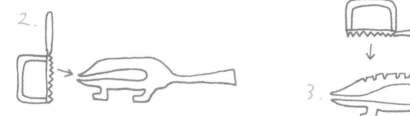

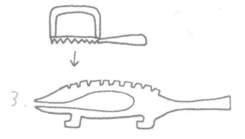

play dress up!

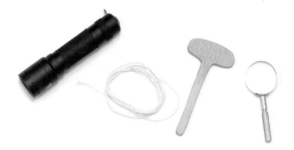

modular headband

This headband allows children to use their creativity to make their own designs, from crowns and dog ears to abstract creations. The first time I showed it to my son, he immediately looked at the pieces and began building. In just a few minutes he introduced me to "rhino-dog"!

materials

Felt: two pieces 16" x 2¼", for the base

Felt scraps, for the attachment pieces (Other
material may be used if you like.)

Velcro

Elastic: 1" width

Faux fur scraps (optional)

Double-sided fusible interfacing (optional)

Scissors and/or rotary cutter

Sewing machine

Headband

1. Using a sewing machine, sew five pieces of Velcro, loop side out and about 3" apart, on one of the felt rectangles for the base.
2. Take the other felt rectangle, place it on the back of the rectangle with the Velcro, and sew along the long edges only.
3. Measure your child's head and determine the length of elastic you'll need to make the headband fit comfortably. Add 1" to the measurement, and cut a length of elastic. (I used 4½" for my three-year-old's headband.) Insert ½" of one end of the elastic into one of the open ends of the headband, and sew along the end of the headband, making sure to sew over the elastic at least a couple of times for strength. Then secure the other end of the elastic to the other end of the headband, making sure to eliminate any twists in the fabric.

headband

1.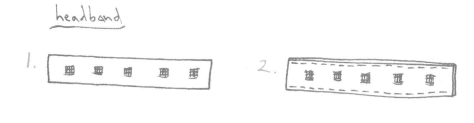

2.

3.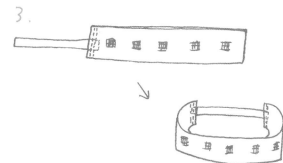

Circular Pieces

1. Make as many circular pieces from scrap material as you'd like. The circles will be stacked, so for each set, I cut three sizes of felt circles: 2¾" diameter, 2" diameter, 1⅜" diameter.
2. Using the sewing machine, sew one piece of Velcro on the back of the largest circle. Make sure the hook side is facing out (opposite that on the headband) so the Velcro attaches.
3. Sew the medium-sized circle on the front of the large circle, then sew the smallest circle on top.

Triangular Crown Pieces

1. Cut one large triangle, two medium triangles, and two small triangles from the fabric scraps. My triangles all had a base of 2¾" and varied in height at 3¼", 4¼", and 5".
2. Sew Velcro pieces on the back of each triangle, hook side facing out.
3. Cut five more triangles slightly smaller than the first five triangles, and sew them on top of the larger ones.

Circular Pieces

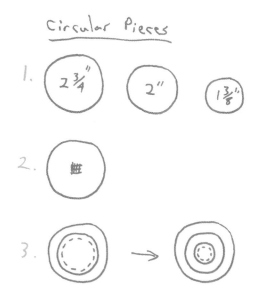

1. $2\frac{3}{4}''$ $2''$ $1\frac{3}{8}''$

2.

3.

triangular crown pieces

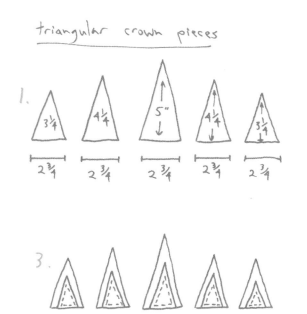

1. $3\frac{1}{4}$ $4\frac{1}{4}$ $5''$ $4\frac{1}{4}$ $3\frac{1}{4}$

$2\frac{3}{4}$ $2\frac{3}{4}$ $2\frac{3}{4}$ $2\frac{3}{4}$ $2\frac{3}{4}$

2.

3.

Doggy Ears

1. Cut faux fur pieces with scissors (preferably outside, because it can get pretty furry) into dog ear shapes. Mine were about 6" in length.

2. After you cut the ear pieces, shake out the fur so the cut edges don't shed.

3. Sew a piece of Velcro, hook side out, on the back of each ear.

Wings

1. Cut two 6" x 6" squares of fabric of your choice.

2. Cut one piece of double-sided fusible interfacing, slightly smaller than 6" x 6".

3. Put the interfacing between the two pieces of fabric, and iron the layers with a hot iron. The interfacing makes the fabric very stiff, so it will stand up. (Be sure to follow the manufacturer's instructions for the best results.)

4. Using scissors, cut the stiff square in half.

5. Cut each piece into a wing shape. Mine were 5¼" tall by 2" wide.

6. Sew a piece of Velcro, hook side out, on the back of each wing.

Doggy Ears

1.   2.    3.

Wings

1.

2.

3.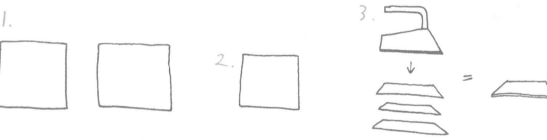

4.

5.

6.

exploration cape

Sometimes a kid really needs a cape. Whether it's a feeling of super-power, a need for a disguise, or simply the search for a little warmth, this handy exploration cape will deliver. It's also a great way to collaborate with your child. You do the sewing and let them create drawings for it.

materials

Fabric for the cape: two pieces 52" x 36"
Fabric for the pockets: one piece, 8½" x 5½"; one
   piece, 5½" x 12"; and one piece, 8" x 13"
Scissors and/or rotary cutter
Sewing machine
Chalk, for drawing the cut lines
Fabric pens
Hair dryer, for drying the pen ink
Velcro
Snap (optional, for pocket)

SNAP POCKET

1. Take the piece of 8½" by 5½" fabric.
2. Fold under the two 5½" ends ½", and sew.
3. Fold the fabric right sides together so
   the bottom edge is about 1" from the top
   edge. Then sew the sides.
4. Turn the bag right-side out. Fold over the
   two side edges of the lid flap ½", and sew.
5. Hammer on a snap or sew on Velcro for
   the pocket flap.

FLASHLIGHT/PEN POCKET

1. Take the piece of 5½" by 12" fabric.
2. Fold under the two 5½" ends about ½",
   and sew.
3. Fold the fabric in half, right sides together,
   and sew along each side.
4. Turn the pocket right-side out.
5. Later, when you sew the pocket to the
   cape, you can sew a vertical stitch up the
   middle of the pocket so it will have two separate compartments.

Snap Pocket

Flashlight/Pen Pocket

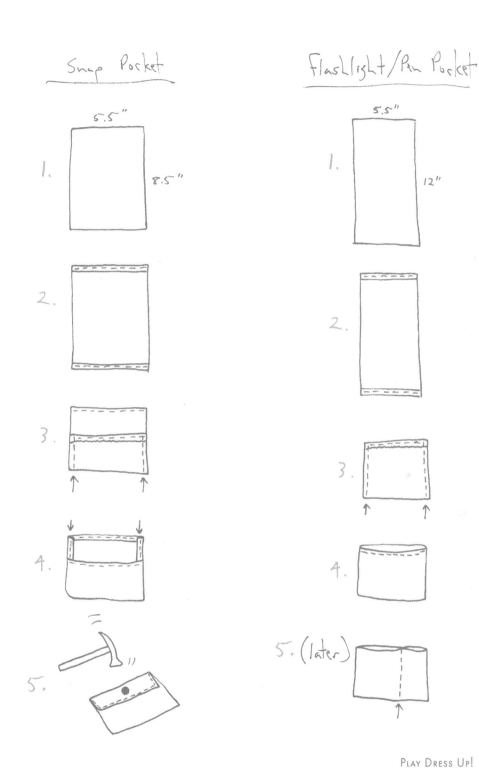

5.5"

8.5"

1.

2.

3.

4.

5.

5.5"

12"

1.

2.

3.

4.

5. (later)

Large Open Pouch

Take the 8" by 13" piece of fabric, and follow steps 2 through 4 of the Flashlight/Pen Pocket.

Cape

1. Take your fabric for the cape, and following the diagram, use chalk to draw the shape of the cape on one of the pieces. Lay that piece on top of the other piece, and cut out both pieces at the same time. Don't worry about getting the dimensions exactly the same as mine. It's just a cape, and when placed around a child's shoulders, the size and dimensions are very forgiving.

2. Place the pockets on the piece of fabric you'll use for the cape lining, and pin them down. Placement is very flexible. Sew the pockets in place along the edges, but don't sew the pocket openings shut. Just lift the opening and sew the underside.

3. Pin the two pieces of fabric, right sides together, and sew around all of the edges except one shoulder.

4. Turn the cape right-side out. Fold in the rough edges on the open shoulder, and sew the opening closed.

5. Sew the Velcro to the cape. I cut three strips of Velcro for each corner and lined them up. This placement made a nice large Velcro surface to adjust the fitting and keep the cape securely attached. Sew the Velcro on the front side of one corner and on the back side of the other corner.

6. Finally, get some fabric pens and have some fun drawing inspiring exploration objects: animals, trees, planets, and so on. If your child is old enough, you can let him or her do the drawing. Or you can use your child's drawings as templates and draw them on the cape yourself. When you finish a drawing, blow it dry with a hot hair dryer to set the ink and keep it from smudging.

7. Help your explorers put on their capes, and start your expedition!

Large Open Pouch

1. 8"
13"

2.

3.

Cape

4.

1. 26"
9"
4"
29"
47"

2.

3.

4.

5. sew on front   sew on back

6.

discoverer's utility belt

Having the right tools when you need them is empowering, and the discoverer's utility belt will be a great help in this area. With it securely around his or her waist, your child can easily carry things like flashlights, pens, a magnifying glass, a prodding stick (for bugs or worms), and pouches and pockets. My kids have a great time using these belts while going on their expeditions, and it somehow gives them an official feeling, which they seem to enjoy a lot.

materials

Fabric for the belt: one piece, 26" x 7"; and one
  piece, 5" x 4½" (I used cotton canvas. Feel free
  to adjust the length of the belt depending on
  the measurements of your child.)
Fabric for the pockets: one piece, 5" x 7"; and one
  piece, 4" x 9"
Velcro
Elastic band: ¾" wide x about 12" long
Zipper: 5"
Sewing machine
Scissors and/or rotary cutter
Wood: thin plywood about 4½" x 2½", for prod-
  ding stick (optional)
Saw (hand coping saw or scroll saw)
Sandpaper
Beeswax polish

BELT

1. Take the larger piece of fabric for the belt,
   and fold it in half lengthwise. Sew along the open
   edge of the length and across one short end.

2. Turn the belt right-side out, and iron it flat.

3. Take the smaller piece of fabric for the
   belt. Fold it in half lengthwise, and sew along
   the length and across one short end. This will
   create the Velcro latch piece.

4. Turn the piece right-side out, and iron it flat.

5. On the large belt, turn under the raw
   edges on the open end ½". Press the edges with
   an iron if you'd like. Insert the rough open end of
   the latch piece into the open end of the belt, and
   sew across both pieces. Sew back and forth a
   few times to make the latch strong and secure.

6. Take two strips of Velcro (about 3½"
   each), and sew them on the back side of the latch
   piece. Then take two more strips, and sew them
   on the front side of the other end of the belt.

Belt

1.

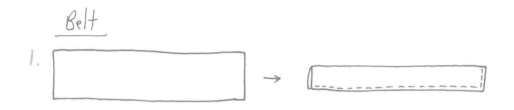

2.

3.

4.

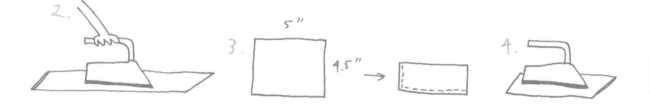

5.

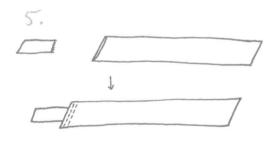

6.

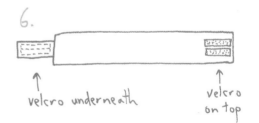

velcro underneath

velcro on top

Zipper Pouch

1. Lay the 5" by 7" piece of fabric right-side up on a table. Place the zipper face down across the top of the short end, aligning the edge of the zipper tape with the raw edge of the fabric. Attach a zipper foot to your sewing machine, and sew across the top of the zipper.
2. Hold on to the unsewn edge of the zipper tape, and fold the opposite side of the fabric over it. The front side of the zipper should be against the right side of the fabric. Now sew across the other side of the zipper.
3. Before sewing the sides, open the zipper up so that it's in the middle of the pouch. Keep the sides aligned so the zipper is flat across the top. This will result in the zipper being on the front of the pouch instead of being right on the top edge. Now sew up both sides of the pocket, sewing over the zipper. (You can put the regular sewing foot back on now.) Sew across the zipper a few times so it's sturdy.
4. Clip the zipper to the width of the pocket. If you've got a metal zipper, you'll need some metal sheers. Turn the pocket right-side out.
5. Sew the pouch on the outside middle of the belt by sewing across the top and bottom of the pouch.

Velcro Pocket

1. Start with the 4" by 9" piece of fabric.
2. Fold under the short ends ½", and sew.
3. Sew a piece of Velcro at the top of one side. Then flip the fabric over, and sew the other piece of Velcro on the bottom of the other side.
4. Fold the bottom of the fabric up, right sides together, leaving about 2" of fabric at the top for the lid flap. Position the folded fabric so the Velcro pieces line up when the lid flap is closed. Once you see that the Velcro pieces will line up, open the flap and sew each side of the pouch.
5. Turn the pouch right-side out. Fold over the rough edges of the lid flap, and sew.
6. Sew the pocket on the belt. Just open the lid of the pouch and sew across the top and bottom. I chose to sew it next to the belt's Velcro latch, so it will be in the front for an easy access pouch.

Zipper Pouch

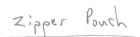

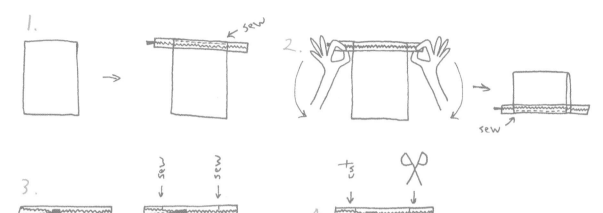

1.

2.

3.

4.

5.

Velcro Pocket

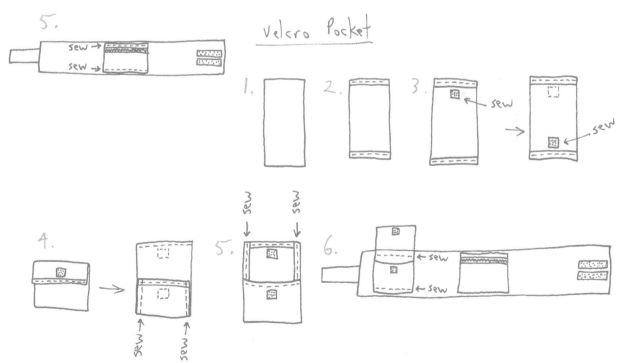

1.

2.

3.

4.

5.

6.

Elastic Loops

The elastic loops are mostly intended for holding tools that will hang down a bit, so it is important that you keep the elastic loops on the sides of the belt (when on the child) so that when children bend and sit down they don't poke themselves with the hanging tools.

1. Sew one end of the elastic to the belt.
   (I attached one 5½" piece of elastic between the two pockets.)
2. Sew the other end to the belt, then sew the middle down.
3. The next set of elastic loops is for smaller tools, so the loops will be smaller. I used another 5½" piece of elastic. I sewed one end to the belt, then kept sewing loops of various sizes all the way to the other end of the elastic. I made five loops in all for this strip.

Prodding Stick

1. Draw a rounded T shape on the wood.
2. Cut out the shape with a saw.
3. Sand it smooth, and cover it with beeswax polish.

Elastic Loops

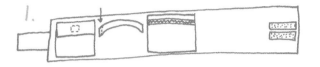

1.

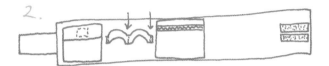

2.

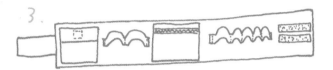

3.

Prodding Stick

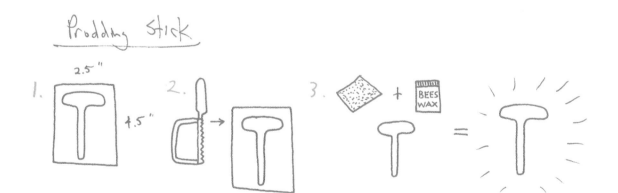

1. 2.5" 4.5"

2.

3. BEES WAX + =

modular leg bands

My kids love pulling on their leg warmers and wearing them around the house. So after making the modular headband, I thought it would be great to make leg bands that would give a child that same sense of creative control. When I showed these to my kids, they immediately started arranging the pieces to create their own leg band designs. The little Velcro pocket is their favorite part. They love having a secret pouch for their small treasures.

materials

Fabric, for the leg bands: four pieces 4" x 9"
Fabric, for the pocket: 4" x 9"
Fabric scraps, for the patches
Scissors and/or rotary cutter
Sewing machine
Velcro: ½" wide x about 22" long
Elastic: 1" wide x about 26" long
Double-sided fusible interfacing (optional)
Snap or Velcro
Fabric pen, for drawing on the patches

Leg Bands

1. Take your four 4" by 9" pieces of fabric. Cut out two 4" by 9" pieces of double-sided fusible interfacing.

2. Put each fusible sheet between two pieces of fabric (you'll have two sandwiches), and press them with a hot iron until the interfacing adheres to the fabric. (Follow the manufacturer's directions for the best results.) The interfacing makes the leg bands stiffer so they hold their shape while being worn. But you could make them without it, too.

3. Trim the edges of the rectangles with scissors or rotary cutter. I chose to round the top corners. The interfacing keeps the edges from fraying too much, but I sewed a zigzag stitch around the edges as well.

4. Take a 9" strip of Velcro, and sew it down the middle of one leg band. Do the same for the other one.

5. Cut two 7" strips of elastic and two 6" strips of elastic. Sew the ends of the 7" strip on the back of one leg band, about 5" from the bottom on each side. Then sew the 6" strip on the back right along the bottom edge on each side. Do the same for the other leg band.

leg Bands

1.

+

fusible   fusible

2.

3.

4.

5.

5"

Attachment Pieces

I mostly used pieces from the Modular Headband (see instructions on page 130). Here are some attachments I made.

Snap Pocket

1. Take the 4" x 9" piece of fabric.
2. Fold over the short ends ½", and sew.
3. Sew a 2"-long piece of Velcro in the middle, just above center, on the right side of the fabric. Make sure it's the kind of Velcro that will stick to the strip on the leg band.
4. Fold the bottom of the fabric, right sides together, leaving about 2" of fabric at the top for the lid flap. Then sew the sides.
5. Turn the pocket right-side out. Fold under the two rough edges of the lid flap, and sew.
6. Hammer on a snap or sew on Velcro to the lid flap.

Drawing Patches

1. Cut out two pieces of material in whatever size you would like for your patch.
2. Sew a piece of Velcro on the back of one piece.
3. Using fabric pens, draw your design on the other piece of fabric. (For this part, if your child is old enough, you could let them do the drawing. The pens I use are non-toxic, but they are still very hard to wash off of clothes, so beware. The other option would be to let the child make a drawing on a piece of paper with regular pens or crayons, and then use that drawing as a template for the fabric drawing you make.)
4. When the drawing is finished, blow the pen ink with a hot hair dryer to set the ink. Once this is done, the ink is permanent and will withstand the washing machine.
5. Layer the two fabric pieces, wrong sides together, and sew around the edges using a zigzag stitch.

Snap Pocket

Drawing Patches

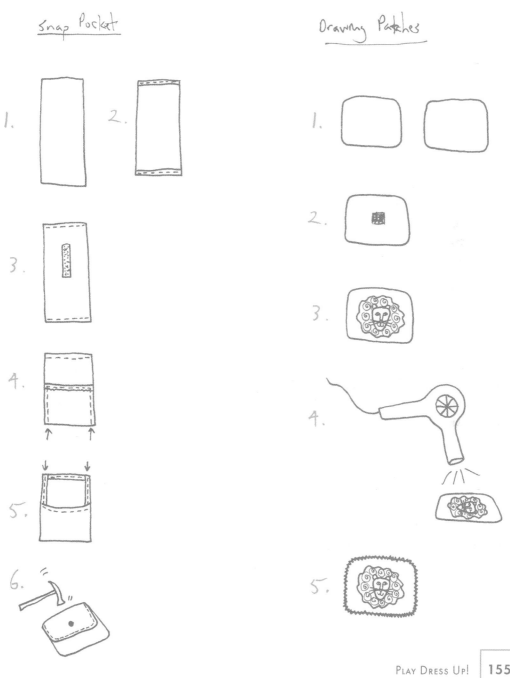

1.
2.
3.
4.
5.
6.

1.
2.
3.
4.
5.

play with art!

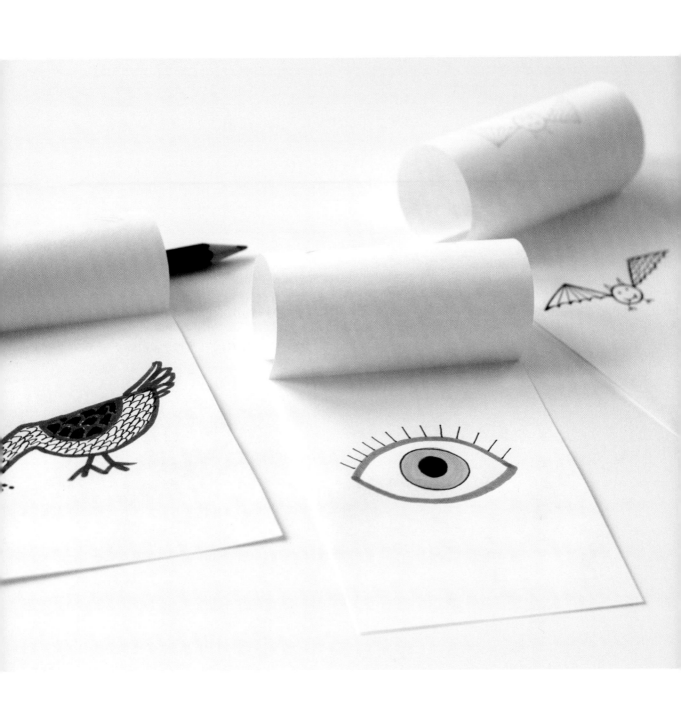

simple paper animation

I used to do this simple paper animation all the time with my friends when I was a kid. I'm not sure who taught me, but everyone I show it to now has never seen it before. At any rate, it's a pretty great trick, and all you need is a pen and paper to try it out yourself!

materials

Pen
Paper (My paper was about 3 ½" by 9".)
Templates (see page 204)

1. Take a long strip of paper, and fold it in half.
2. Using the templates or your own designs, draw the bottom layer first so you can trace over it while making the top drawing. (See page 12 on how to transfer the templates.) Also, leave at least 1" of blank paper at the bottom of your drawing so the curled paper won't slide off of your pencil as you're moving it up and down.
3. Fold down the top piece of paper, and draw the second part of the animation. Trace the drawing underneath so that the animation is smooth.
4. Roll the top sheet of paper around your pen to create the curl.
5. Keep the pen inside the curl of the top paper, and quickly move your pen up and down over and over to bring your animation to life!

1.

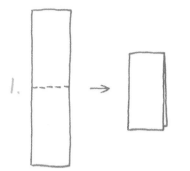

2.

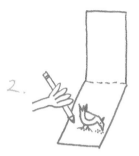

3.

4.

5.

dress-up drawings

While drawing with the kids one morning, I thought it would be fun to take some fabric scraps and cut them into clothes so we could dress up the drawings. My kids were busy drawing while telling me what fabric they wanted for the clothes they were envisioning. I had a great time dressing up my own drawings, too.

materials

Paper
Pen
Fabric scraps
Scissors
Glue (optional)

1. Draw your figures on the paper.
2. Cut out clothing from the fabric, and place it on the drawings.
3. When finished, you can either keep the dress-up clothes in a container for next time or glue them to the drawings to make the art more permanent. Then you can even cut out the figures to make paper dolls.

1.  →

2.   →

3.  or +  →

drawing with vintage buttons

After receiving the marvelous gift of vintage buttons from my wife's grandmother, I tried to come up with a simple way to start putting them to good use. I loved playing around with the simple concept of making some drawings and leaving blank areas on which the kids can place buttons. It's very fun to try different buttons in different places. Get ready for endless creative options!

materials

Paper
Pen
Buttons
Templates (see page 205)

1. Using the templates or your own designs that involve circles of some kind, create some drawings, but leave the circles out of the drawing.

2. Now place various buttons on the drawings where the circles would be. Remember to try swapping out different kinds of buttons to change the look of your drawings!

1.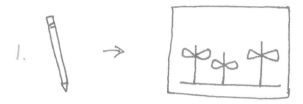

2.  or

record sleeve art tote

I love vintage records, but sometimes they wear out. Or worse, they turn out to be a little too scratched to play. So why not use the cool cover to make your child an art supply tote. It's fun to make, recyclable, works well, and you get major style points.

materials

Record sleeve
Masking tape
Scissors or craft knife
Elastic: ½" wide x about 6½" long (A rubber band
   will also work.)

1. Hold the record sleeve with the open side up,
   then cut open the two sides so it will lie flat in
   one long piece.
2. Make an additional fold, about 1½"
   away from the existing fold.
3. With the record sleeve flat, trim the
   sides, leaving 9" from the fold on each side.
   (When you fold your tote up, each side will be
   9" tall.)
4. Fold the tote together. Toward the top,
   use a craft knife to cut out a hole for a handle.
   I cut a rectangle that was about 4" by 1".
5. Take the strips that you cut off in step 3,
   and fold the edges twice, then tape them to
   the inside of the tote. The length and placement of your strips can vary, depending on the
   size of your art supplies.
6. Finally, you can use some elastic to
   make another place to secure some supplies.
   Just take a strip of elastic, and tape the ends
   down. Done!
7. Now pack up your art supplies, and find a
   nice place to do some drawing!

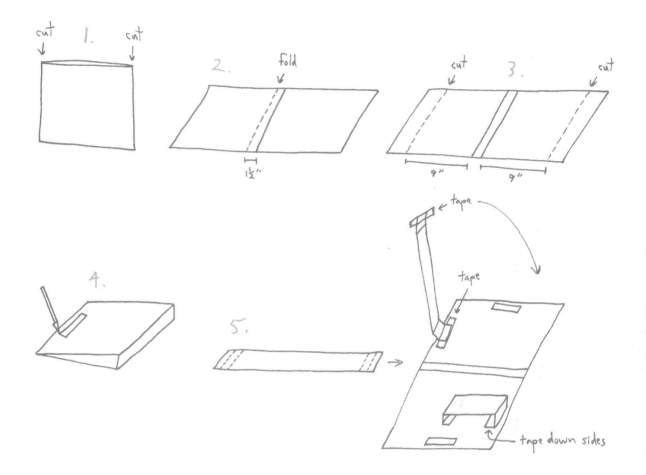

1.

cut   cut

2.

fold

1½"

3.

cut   cut

9"   9"

4.

5.

tape

tape

tape down sides

6.

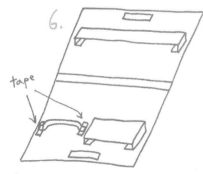

tape

7.

spinning sculpture

Let your kids experiment with physics while having fun at the same time. This spinning sculpture has wooden weights on each end that can slide down the wire. Balance the weights perfectly and achieve a longer spin.

materials

Wood (almost any small wood scraps will work)

Wire (I used some steel welding rod, but any sturdy wire will do.)

Needle-nose pliers

Drill

One nail (The nail needs to be long enough to go through the top pieces and into the base. My nail was 1¼" long.)

Two buttons

Sandpaper

Paint (optional)

Beeswax polish

1. Take a 12" length of wire and, holding the middle of the wire with pliers, wrap the sides to create a loop in the center of the wire.

2. Gather some wood scraps, and sand any rough edges. You'll need a piece for the base (my base was ¾" thick and 2½" square), a piece for the middle stand (I used a small 1¼"-diameter circle—painted white in the photo), and two pieces for the weights on the ends (I cut two pieces off a ¾"-thick stick of wood).

3. Find a drill bit the same size or a little smaller than the thickness of your wire. Drill holes in the two wooden weights so they can slide up and down the wire. Then drill a hole through the center of the middle piece.

4. Sand all the pieces until they are smooth. Paint the pieces if you'd like, and cover them with beeswax when they are dry.

5. Find two smooth buttons. The buttons will create less friction and allow the wire to spin longer. Put a nail through one buttonhole, then through the loop in the middle of the wire, then through the second button. Pound the end of the nail into the hole in the wooden middle piece. Then pound the nail all the way into the wooden base so everything is secure.

6. Slide wooden weights onto the wires, and use the pliers to bend a loop on the ends of the wire to keep the wooden weights from falling off.

7. Spin!

1.

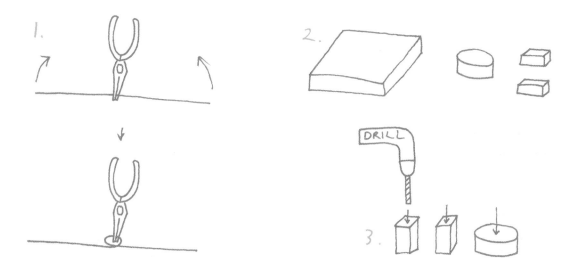

2.

DRILL

3.

4.

5.

6.

7.

wall hanging paper and wire sculptures

Making a little wall hanging sculpture is a great way to bring children's drawings to life. They can draw whatever they'd like, and you can attach it to the wire. You'll probably need to do the wire bending, unless your child is old enough.

Note: It's always a good idea to wear safety glasses when bending wire.

materials

Wire: 18-gauge, 18"-long stem wire (You can find
    packs of it at most any craft store.)
Paper
Pens or paint
Scissors
Tape or glue
Needle-nose pliers
Nail, to hang the sculpture
Templates (see page 204–6)

1. Using the pliers, bend a small loop at the end
of the wire (for the nail to go through). Then
make an angular bend about 1" away from the
hole.

2. Slide your thumb and forefinger down
the wire, bending it slightly to create a small
arch.

3. With the pliers, bend a little design into
the other end of the wire. (I did a spiral for the
owl sculpture and made some wavelike bends
for the fish.)

4. Take a piece of paper, and fold it in half.
Using the template or your own design, draw
a figure on the paper. (See page 12 on how to
transfer the templates.) For the owl, I drew the
outline so that the bottom of the feet lined up
against the fold of the paper. Cut out the shape.

5. Color or draw on both sides of the
figure with paint or pens.

6. For the owl, open up the figure and apply
a thick layer of glue. Wrap the paper around
the wire, and stick the paper together. Lay
the owl flat while the glue dries. For the fish,
I used a single piece of paper and painted
both sides, then tied some thread to the end of
the wire and attached the fish with a piece of
clear tape.

7. Then nail the figures to the wall!

1.

2.

3.

4.

5.

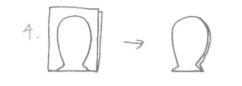

6.

7.

modern alphabet game

At the beach one weekend, we had a great time finding smooth rocks in the sand. While I was painting them, an idea for a game came into my mind. My three-year-old twins had begun recognizing letters in the alphabet, so I was excited to try this game with its blend of learning, creating art, and practicing social graces, like waiting to take turns. The twins loved the game! They were excited to earn their rocks and add to their artistic creations on the boards, all the while learning their letters.

materials

Bag of letters (from Scrabble or similar tile word
   game)
Plywood: two pieces of ¼" plywood in sizes of
   your choosing (I made two boards that mea-
   sured 11" x 5 ½" each.)
Rocks (I used 24 rocks.)
Fabric (Mine was 10 ½" in diameter.)
Saw (I used a scroll saw.)
Sandpaper
Paint
Beeswax polish

1. Use a saw to cut the game boards. I made two
   boards that measured 11" by 5 ½" each, but
   your boards can be any size you like.
2. Sand the boards so they are smooth.
3. Paint a design on the boards. I used
   black and white acrylic paint. Try to make
   your design have obvious spaces to place the
   rocks.
4. Cut out a piece of fabric on which to
   place the rocks. I made a circle, 10 ½" in diameter. I used a natural denim fabric and left the
   edges raw.
5. Paint designs on the rocks. I created
   eight rock designs and made three sets of different colors with those designs.
6. Get your bag of letters, and play!

How to Play

To play the game, arrange the rocks in the middle on
a circle of fabric. Each child takes a turn by drawing a letter from inside the bag. If they can correctly
identify the letter, they get to choose a rock and
place it on their board. When their board is full, they
win! (Each child can keep playing until they all win!)

Variation for Older Children

Each child gets eight letters. If they can lay out a
word, they get a rock. Then they draw more tiles
to replace the ones they used. This way, older and
younger children can play together and all can
enjoy the same game. You could even create math
tiles (2 + 2 = ___), or object tiles for vocabulary, or
whatever needs to be learned.

1.

2.

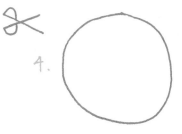

3.

4.

5.

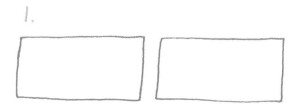

shadow box theater

I have great memories, as a kid, of putting on magic shows, puppet shows, and skits with my sisters and cousins. We would perform for all of the adults in the family and charge 10¢ admission. It was great to get the approval and response from the audience, and it gave us kids a feeling of pride. Recently, I've been wanting to do shadow puppets with my kids, but I never got around to tacking up a big sheet and setting up the lights. Then I thought of a small and simple way to do shadow puppets with this portable cardboard box theater. In just a few minutes, you'll have your own mini theater, too, so you can put on a shadow puppet show tonight!

materials

Cardboard box, any size

Flashlight

Fabric, to hang over the front of your box (Any lightweight and light-colored fabric will work. I used an old pillowcase that needed repurposing. Even a large sheet of white paper would be fine.)

Aluminum foil

Tape (I used double-sided clear tape and clear packing tape.)

Black construction paper (Any stiff paper or scraps from the cardboard box would also work.)

Templates (see page 206)

1. Cut off all four flaps on the open end of the box.
2. In the bottom corner along one side, cut a hole for the flashlight then two long, narrow notches on either side for the puppet sticks.
3. Line the inside of the box with aluminum foil, and secure the foil in place with double-sided tape.
4. Drape the piece of fabric (or paper) over the open end of the box, and secure it with some thick tape along the top and bottom of the box. (I used clear packing tape.) Then insert the flashlight into the flashlight hole.
5. Using the templates or your own designs, draw some puppet shapes onto thick dark paper and cut them out. (See page 12 on how to transfer the templates.)
6. With the leftover cardboard (from the lid flaps) cut a few thin strips for handles and tape the paper puppets onto them.
7. Now turn off the lights, and put on a puppet show!

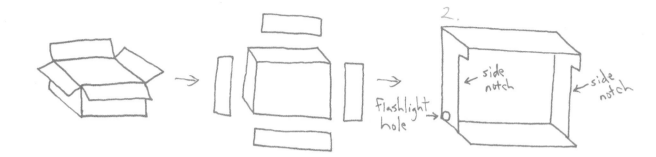

2.

← side notch

→ side notch

Flashlight hole →

3.

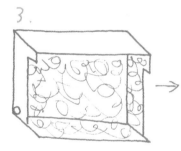

4.

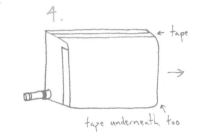

← tape

→

tape underneath too

5.

6.

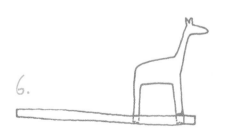

7.

templates

For instructions on how to transfer these designs to your projects, see page 12. PDFs of these templates are also available to download at www.madebyjoel.com and www.Shambhala.com/madetoplay. Please use the templates from this book for your own personal use.

Portable Zoo Animals

Actual size templates

Animal Finger Puppets

Actual size templates

Small Wooden Animals

Actual size templates

Paper Barn and Animals

Enlarge by 400%

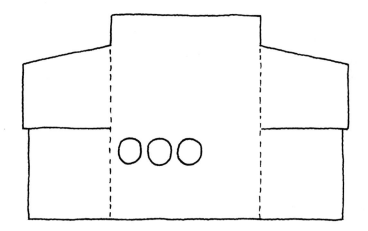

Actual size templates

Embroidered Pillow Doll

Actual size template

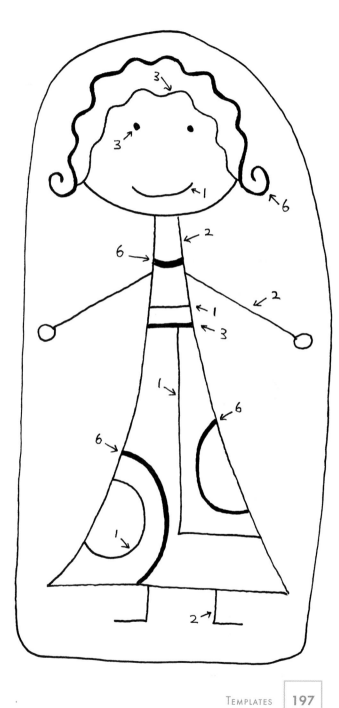

Wooden Sleeping Doll

Actual size template

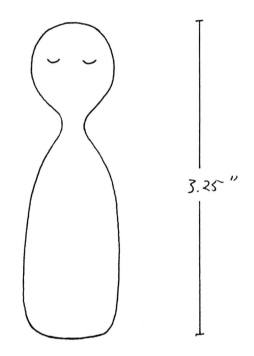

3.25 ”

slotted building discs

Actual size template

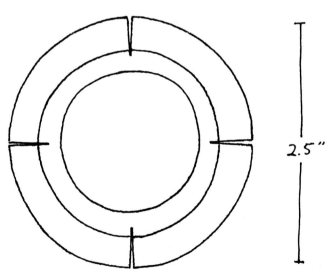

2.5 ”

small Wooden Trucks

Actual size templates

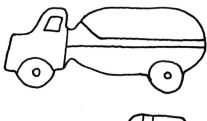

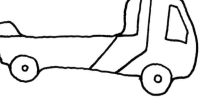

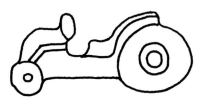

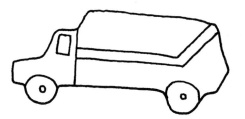

Wooden Nature Scene

Enlarge by 175%

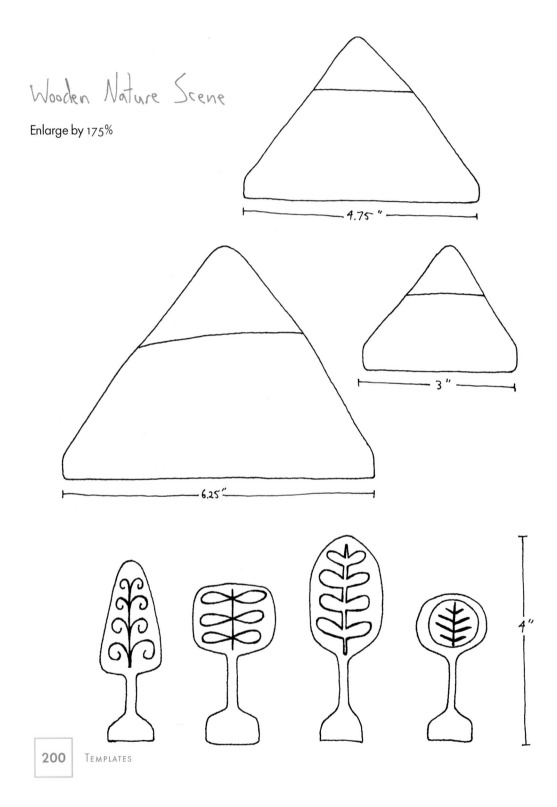

4.75 "

6.25 "

3 "

4 "

Sewn Trumpet

Enlarge by 240%

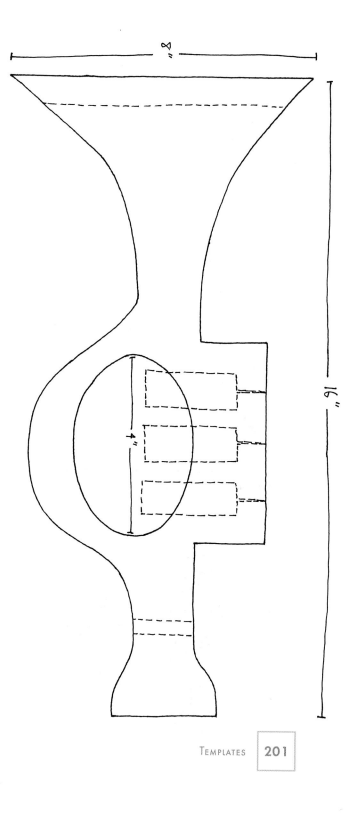

Fabric Instruments

Enlarge by 650%

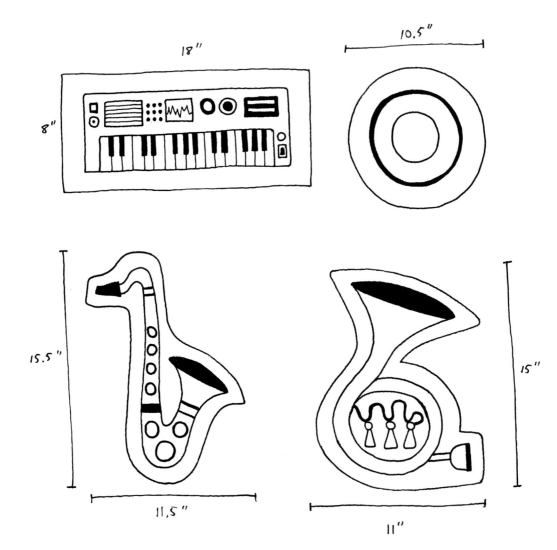

18"

8"

10.5"

15.5"

11.5"

15"

11"

Wooden Guiro

Enlarge by 140%

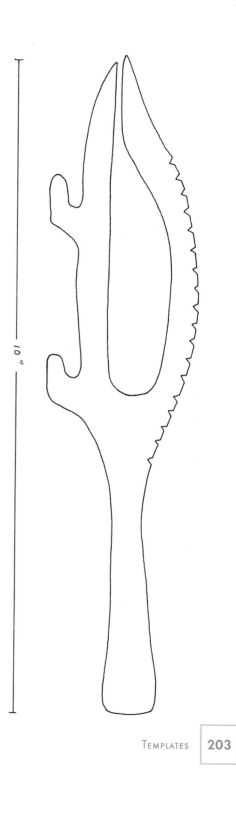

10"

Simple Paper Animation

Actual size templates

Paper and Wire Sculptures

Enlarge 150%

3"

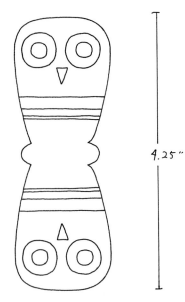

4.25"

Drawing with Vintage Buttons

Enlarge by 200%

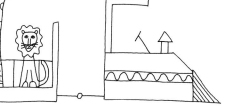

Shadow Box Theater

4"

4"

Enlarge by 160%

5.5"

7"

about the author

Joel Henriques is fascinated by color, shape, and craftsmanship. He was drawn to painting as a child, inspired by his grandmother, a painter herself. She spent hours showing Joel the paintings of Matisse, Picasso, Miró, and many others. Through these and her own paintings, she taught him ideas about color and design, and eventually coached him on his earliest paintings.

These childhood experiences were lasting. Creating art became a passion for Joel at a young age, which led him to pursue a B.A. in fine art and philosophy. After college, Joel continued to focus heavily on developing his design style and technique.

Becoming a parent was, for Joel, another way of looking at art in the world. As a young child himself, he made many of his own toys. As a father, he began making toys for his young twins. He began to see that a beautiful, minimal, well-crafted object allowed his children to use and develop their own imaginations, rather than having an object tell them how they must play with it.

Moved by his children's interaction with art, Joel began documenting these crafts on his blog, *Made By Joel*. Creating art for children, and for the child in everyone, is a powerful thing. The response to Joel's blog has been amazing, reaching people all over the world.

Joel lives with his wife and three-year-old twins in Portland, Oregon. See more of his crafts at www.madebyjoel.com, and see more of his art at www.joelhenriques.com.

ROOST BOOKS
An imprint of Shambhala Publications, Inc.
Horticultural Hall
300 Massachusetts Avenue
Boston, Massachusetts 02115
roostbooks.com

9 8 7 6 5 4 3 2 1

First Edition
Printed in the United States of America

⊗This edition is printed on acid-free paper that meets the American National
Standards Institute Z39.48 Standard.
♻ Shambhala Publications makes every effort to print on recycled paper.
For more information please visit www.shambhala.com.

Distributed in the United States by Random House, Inc.,
and in Canada by Random House of Canada Ltd

Designed by Daniel Urban-Brown

Library of Congress Cataloging-in-Publication Data
Henriques, Joel.
Made to play!: handmade toys and crafts for growing imaginations /
Joel Henriques.— 1st ed.
p.   cm.
ISBN 978-1-59030-912-4 (pbk.: alk. paper)
1. Toy making. I. Title.
TT174.H46 2011
688.7'2—dc22
2011006013